SCRAP BONANZA!

2-for-1 Quilts

...make a second quilt with the scraps from the first...

by
Linda Halpin

RCW
PUBLISHING COMPANY

Dedication:

to Gary, Corey, and Amanda,

who are always there to help, make suggestions, and support me.

Acknowledgments:

Susan Sterritt
who machine quilted my scrap quilts with great skill, enthusiasm, and speed
and
Judith Youngman
who never fails to see my designs in a new light that leads me down
an unexplored path

Credits:

Photography by Stephen J. Appel Photography, Vestal, New York

Lynn Balassone
RCW graphic designer

Cover Quilt:

Stacked Bricks
owned by Corey Robert Halpin
Made by Linda Halpin
Quilted by Susan Sterritt

Scrap Bonanza!
2 - for - 1 Quilts ©
© 1994 by Linda Halpin
Rebecca C. Wilber Publishing Company
RR #3 Old Post Lane
Columbia Cross Roads, Pennsylvania 16914-9535
717-549-3331

ISBN 0-9627646-6-3

Table of Contents:

How To Use This Book:

Scrap Bonanza is presented in two parts. In Part One, rotary cut pieces are cut and used to construct a scrap quilt. The leftover pieces create a second scrap quilt that is totally different from the first.

In Part Two, the Nine Patch block is explored, ranging from making blocks with specific color placement to different pattern-changing ways to set them together. Begin with a stack of Nine Patch blocks and see where they lead you. The possibilities are endless!

Fabric selection techniques are discussed in the opening chapter, giving you guidelines for combining your fabrics to create a wide range of colorations, moods, and themes. These methods work equally well for scrap quilts and quilts with a specific color palette.

All patterns are accompanied by a reference chart listing yardage requirements for the various areas of each pattern to assist you should you need to purchase fabric to round out your collection for any area of the quilt.

Charts for each quilt include information for wall/crib, twin/single, full/double, and queen size quilts, including how much 'drop over the sides' and 'pillow tuck-in' each size allows for.

Throughout the book you will find *HINT HIGHLIGHTS* to help make your quiltmaking more enjoyable. While geared specifically to quiltmaking, many of the hints are also invaluable in other areas of machine stitching.

And finally, the bibliography at the end of *Scrap Bonanza* lists sources of information on more scrap quilts, quilting, and finishing. Whether left as a quilt top* or a quilted quilt, you are sure to find patterns here to entice you.

*It's never an unfinished project... think of it as a 'work in progress'.

A word of warning, however.... 2 - for - 1 Scrap Quilts can take over your quiltmaking life. The joy of creating something beautiful out of scraps is great fun in itself, but to see a second quilt blossom out of the scraps of scraps makes it even more exciting! So take care, and ENJOY!

Introduction:

Scrap Bonanza takes a new look at how scrap quilts are made. Rather than cutting out prescribed numbers of specific templates, use your rotary cutter to cut piles of scraps in a variety of strips, squares, and rectangles. Speed piecing techniques are then employed to create wonderful scrap quilts.

The special bonus to this method is that not only does it free you of the constraining mindset of template requirements, but the leftover pieces from the first quilt can be used to create a second quilt that is totally different. That's two quilts for the price of one. The more fabrics you use, the more your quilts will sparkle, making room to add more fabrics to your collection.

Who knows how many quilts are already in your fabric stash just waiting to come to life!

Characteristics of Scrap Quilts:

Through color choice and fabric selection, you can set the mood of your scrap quilt. For example:

* Ivory backgrounds can be reminiscent of antique quilts. To give the illusion of the extensive quilting often found on antique quilts, incorporate 'white-on-white' and 'printed muslins' in your fabric collection.

* Bright, vivid, clear colors set a happy mood.

* Solid black backgrounds give the sophistication of Amish quilts.

* Homespuns and plaids cut without regard to the woven pattern give an antique, homey flavor, while the same fabrics cut on grain give a tailored appearance.

* Darker backgrounds, particularly browns, blacks, and blues, are typical of the 1880's-1890's.

* Pastels were popular in the 1930's.

* The combination of solids and tiny prints is typical of the 1970's.

* Strategic placement of specific design elements speaks of the 1980's.

* Integration of hand-dyed fabrics with commercial fabrics creates a contemporary flair.

In studying antique scrap quilts, there are several characteristics that distinguish them from other quilts. Recognizing these qualities can help you create a scrap quilt that has antique flavor.

Quilters were not afraid to use every kind of print. They used stripes, plaids, dots, and large prints, as well as small prints and solids.

It was OK if color didn't match. Many scrap quilts were made from what was on hand, not what was purchased. You will often find bits of really ugly fabric hidden in a scrap quilt. Used in large quantities it would glare, but woven into a scrap quilt, it lends charm and vitality.

Scrap quilts are very random in their nature. Not every piece is planned, as in many of today's quilts. This is one instance where you have to let go of that organized side of yourself and let things develop on their own. Quilt blocks are created by random placement of fabrics, but the positioning of the blocks in the quilt can be planned, allowing you some control over the finished product. Use of a flannel board allows you to do this easily.

A flannel board is an expanse of napped fabric on which you can play with the position of a quilt's components before they are sewn together. It can be something as simple as a one yard length of flannel pinned up on a wall, or even pinned up to your curtains. I prefer a 2 yard length of fabric, positioned horizontally on the wall, as this gives me room to lay out blocks for a variety of sizes of quilts prior to sewing the quilt blocks together.

The advantages to using a flannel board are many. Blocks can be laid out on a flannel board by simply patting them in place. They will adhere to the flannel, thereby allowing you to play with block arrangement without having to rip blocks apart if you want to try a new arrangement.

When arranging blocks for their final placement in a quilt, stand back to get an overall view of the image they create. Are the colors distributed throughout the quilt in a pleasing fashion? Are the light areas of the quilt scattered throughout the quilt surface? This will keep the eye moving over the quilt to create greater visual interest. Are there colors that you wanted in your quilt that are not in there? As you make additional blocks, you can add any desired fabrics.

In the making of any of the quilts in *Scrap Bonanza,* the blocks for each pattern are the same size, regardless of what size quilt you are making. If you decide to make the quilt larger than originally planned, and you choose a new fabric that hasn't been used in previously made blocks, you can integrate them with the original grouping of blocks as you lay them out on the flannel board.

Standing back to review your arrangement of blocks before stitching them together is vital to the overall visual effect of the finished quilt. If your work area is not large enough for you to physically stand back and look at your layout, try looking at

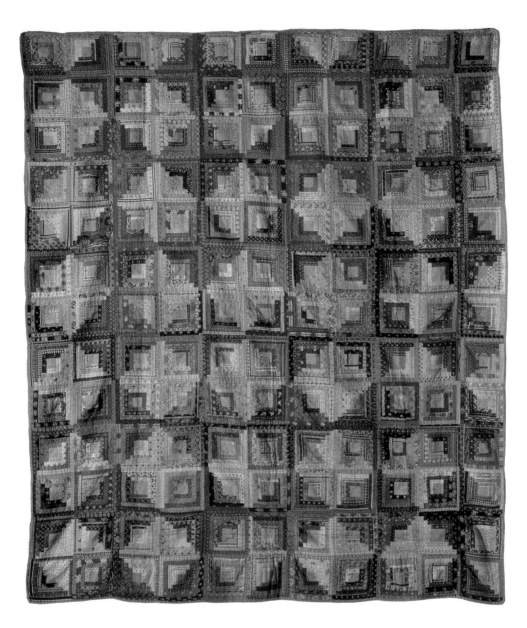

Log Cabin Quilt
68 3/4" x 81 1/4"
Made c. 1860-80
Collection of the Chemung County Historical Society,
Elmira, NY

The variety of fabrics used in this quilt are typical of
those used in quilts from the 1860's - 1880's.
Note the combination of scales of design in the prints.

it through your camera or through the wrong end of binoculars. Either of these methods will give you the effect of standing back several feet. Any areas that are too light, too dark, too similar, or too jarring will stand out. Rearrange the blocks now, before they are sewn together, to minimize the offending view, or to highlight a feature that attracts you.

Colors:

While fabrics in scrap quilts are random in nature, you can still choose an overall color scheme before you begin to give your quilt a sense of unity. There are several fabric selection tricks you may want to use to do this.

One is to choose a multicolored fabric you really like and use it as a 'shopping list' for the colors you want in your quilt. Gather up a grocery bag full of scraps in that range of colors. To retain the scrap feeling, remember to use a variety of values (lights, mediums, and darks) of the colors on your shopping list, and a range of visual textures in your fabrics (by including several scales of design... small, medium, large prints, geometrics, etc.)

Be sure to have good contrast (a variety of lights, mediums, and darks) so your patchwork pattern will show up well. If you would like to also incorporate that fabric that gives you your 'shopping list' in your quilt, remember that this is a scrap quilt. Do not center the motifs of the print when you cut templates, but rather, cut them randomly, so the design appears to float in and out of the blocks.

Another source of inspiration for selecting color ranges is to set up a 'pretty picture file'. Keep in it such things as magazine pictures, post cards, photos, gift cards.... anything that appeals to you either because of the colors, patterns, choice of quilting pattern, border treatment... whatever. Browse through this from time to time to keep these ideas fresh in your mind. They may provide the seed which starts your next project.

Studying quilts from different time periods is also a source of ideas for color combination. Each time period had colors characteristic to it. As different periods may appeal to you, this may be a deciding factor in what range of colors you work in.

reds/greens:	mid 1800's
browns/rusts/blues:	1870's - 80's
dark prints:	1890's-1925
(particularly dark blues, blacks, and grays)	
pastels:	1920's-1930's
earth tones:	1970's
blues/browns:	early 1980's
navy/burgundy:	mid 1980's

There are some fabrics that were characteristic of antique scrap quilts that you may like to build into your quilt. These included white backgrounds with tiny black figures, bubble gum pink, shirting stripes, and tiny checks.

While scrap quilts contain a large number of fabrics, you can create some sense of order by choosing one particular color for one position in your block. The background position, for example, may all be light tan, but use several light tans/printed muslins in that position. This tends to retain the scrap look of the quilt, but with some sense of order and a great deal of texture.

If you have fabrics that are too garish or bright for the desired effect, try dying the fabrics to tone them down. Tea-dying gives an orangey-brown while coffee-dying gives a reddish-brown.

> **HINT:** *To tea-dye fabric, brew a large pot of tea using 4 - 5 tea bags. Remove tea bags from pot. Pre-wet your fabric before adding it to the pot. This will help insure that the tea is absorbed evenly. Stir the fabric in the pot until it is slightly darker than the desired shade. Remove fabric from the pot. Rinse in cold water to remove excess tea. Squeeze out excess moisture. Heat-set the stain by placing the fabric in the dryer or ironing the fabric dry (take care not to scorch the fabric). Once the fabric is dry, wash it to stop the reaction of the tea's tannic acid with the fibers of the fabric.*

Remember that you can nearly double the fabric choices you have to work with by using the wrong side of your fabrics. This not only increases your color options, but adds subtle shading not otherwise available.

One or two blocks with high contrast scattered throughout the quilt will capture attention and keep the eye moving throughout the quilt, making it more interesting to look at. This could be accomplished either with some of the ugly fabrics mentioned earlier, or with bright colors. You don't need many of them, but a few will add greatly to the spark in your scrap quilt. Choosing to include a bright or ugly fabric on purpose is probably the hardest part about making a scrap quilt.

Remember to use fabrics that will give your quilt:

* contrast: light vs. dark....if the fabrics are too similar in value (lightness or darkness), the edges of the design will blur together.

* texture: vary the scale of the designs printed on the cloth. Include solids, small prints (either of which could serve as a backdrop to the bolder fabrics), medium prints, and large prints, geometrics, plaids, stripes, and so on.

100% cottons are easiest to work with. They press well. (Just because this is a scrap quilt does not eliminate the need for precision piecing and pressing.) Including fabrics that are blends may lead to problems when you press. A too-hot-iron may melt some of the blend fabrics to the point where the edges shrivel up.

As in all quilt projects, fabrics should be prewashed. This removes chemical sizing which, when ironed, releases fumes that are damaging to your lungs, hurts your eyes, and makes the fabric more difficult to sew through. Skipped stitches in machine sewing are often caused by the sizing on unwashed fabrics.

Borders:

In studying antique scrap quilts, you will notice that many scrap quilts were pieced out to the edges of the quilt, with no borders (after all, borders require lots of yardage), or the borders were pieced. One thing borders did not have in scrap quilts was mitered corners. This leaves you open to a variety of corner treatments which are easier and faster than mitered corners, from borders that are attached first to the sides of the quilt then to the top and bottom of the quilt, to borders that repeat one of the block elements in the corners.

Be sure to look at the edge treatment of the quilts shown in *Scrap Bonanza*. There is no right or wrong way to do borders on scrap quilts. The choice is yours. Have fun with it.

Yardage Requirements:

You will find a yardage chart for each of the patterns in this book. Yardages are given for wall/crib, twin/single, full/double, and queen sizes.

Yardages are listed for various positions in the pattern. If, for example, you don't currently have many light fabrics and need to buy fabric to supplement your collection, the chart lists how much total yardage you need for the light position in the quilt. Also listed is the amount of fabric needed if being purchased for the particular borders shown on each quilt, and the size square needed for binding.

All yardage calculations have been done with 42" wide fabric so as to accommodate some of the narrower designer fabrics now on the market.

Cutting for Machine Piecing:

Construction methods in *Scrap Bonanza* are done with a sewing machine. Several speed techniques will be used throughout the book.

Pieces will be cut for these quilts using a rotary cutter, building in the seam allowances as you cut. In this manner, you may cut through four layers of cloth at a time (with more than that, you tend to lose accuracy, and although this method is fast, you must still maintain accuracy to get good results.)

1/4" seams are built into all cutting measurements.

Fabrics:

Divide your fabrics into two piles according to their 'color value' (how light or dark they are). Place lights in one pile and darks in the other pile. Fabrics that are neither light nor dark (mediums) can go in either pile. Do not eliminate mediums, as they are a vital link between the lights and darks and help to add zest to your color range.

HINT: Where to use 'medium fabrics':
When using mediums in the light position of a quilt block, pair them up with a really dark fabric to make them appear light.
When using them in the dark position, pair them up with a really light fabric to make them appear dark.

Each pattern has a listing of how many of each shape is required for the finished piece. Use this as a guide to let you know if you are approaching having the required number of pieces cut out or not.

Do not cut all of the pieces before you begin sewing. This can be tedious, boring, and can cause you to abandon the project before you even get to the fun part! Besides, once you get piecing, you may discover that you need to add a particular fabric in order to obtain the zip you want in your quilt.

Cut out a pile of pieces, then get to the fun part of sewing. After you have sewn a few blocks together, you will see how the fabrics are working together, and this can act as a guide to let you know which fabrics you want to cut into for the next batch of blocks. Continue cutting and sewing, building your quilt by placing blocks on the flannel board until it is the desired size.

Once you have the required number of blocks, play with their arrangement. Stand back for an overall view. Make changes now if necessary so as to avoid having to do 'the frog stitch' (rip it ... rip it).

Setting Up Your Work Area:

There are several things you can do to make your working environment more enjoyable and optimize your time.

* Be sure you are working in good light. Poor light contributes to fatigue and mistakes. Portable clamp-on lights are an inexpensive solution to providing more light for your work area.

* You will have four basic work stations: cutting, sewing, pressing, and a flannel board. At the very least, put all four areas in the same room. This eliminates wasted time traveling between stations. A secretary's chair on wheels is perfect for your sewing room. It allows you to travel from sewing to pressing easily and gives you the back support you need.

* Position your ironing board at right angles to your sewing machine at the same level as your sewing machine table. One of the key elements in successful quiltmaking is accurate pressing as you work.

* If your sewing area can not accommodate a full size ironing board, try a child's ironing board (the size is just right for pressing quilt blocks and their components as you work), or make a portable ironing board by covering a cardboard insert from a bolt of fabric with an old towel.

* Set up a disposable trash bin by folding back a cuff on a paper bag and taping it to your work table. The cuff helps to hold the bag open. When the bag is full, toss it out. There's nothing more discouraging at the end of a work session than having to clean up. This helps to keep your work area neater and cuts down on cleanup time.

Supplies:

* *neutral thread:* choosing a thread color that blends well with your fabric assortment will prevent the need to change thread colors as you work. Light to medium shades of tan or gray are very versatile and work well for scrap quilts.

HINT: Use the same brand of thread for the upper and bobbin threads for best stitch quality. Different brands of thread in these two positions is sometimes the cause of skipped stitches.

* *pins:* slender pins approximately 1" in length work best for matching seams in patchwork. The shafts of longer pins get in the way and reduce

your flexibility. Work with pins no larger around than a size 8 quilting needle. Fatter shafts tend to puncture holes in the fabric.

* *bobbins:* Wind two or three bobbins in your choice of thread before you begin. Machine piecing goes through thread quickly. You will be glad for the convenience of pre-wound bobbins.

* *flannel board:* You will find this an especially helpful tool for working with scrap quilt blocks and the various ways of setting them together.

* *fabrics:* Pull together an assortment of scrap fabrics. Divide fabrics into lights and darks. Medium fabrics can be placed in either pile. If using a medium fabric in a 'light position', place it next to a really dark fabric when stitching. That will make the medium fabric appear lighter. If using a medium fabric in a 'dark position', place it next to a really light fabric when stitching. That will make the medium fabric appear darker.

Cutting Fabrics:

As described earlier, do not cut all of the required pieces at once. Cut assorted scraps of light, medium, and dark fabrics into the required shapes. Begin the construction of your quilt blocks. See how your fabrics are working together. Placing completed blocks up on the flannel board will give you an indication as to what values (light, medium, or dark), scales of design (small, medium, or large), and/or colors are missing from your collection. Additional pieces can be cut as needed as the quilt top grows.

Begin by straightening one edge of the fabric:
* Fold long pieces of fabric, aligning selvage edges, so the expanse of fabric being cut is in the 12" - 18" range. Place fabric on the cutting mat.

* Position one of the perpendicular lines on the ruler even with the folds, with the edge of the ruler near the raw edge of fabric that needs to be straightened.

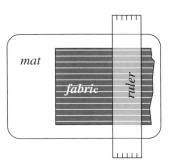

If you are right-handed:
position the edge being straightened to the right (as shown above).
If you are left handed:
position the edge being straightened to the left.

* Hold the ruler firmly in place, keeping finger tips away from the edge of the ruler. To begin your cut, start BELOW the folded edge of the fabric, placing the blade of your cutter along the edge of the ruler, and cut away from you, allowing the blade of the cutter to ride against the edge of the ruler as a cutting guide.

* If the piece required is, for example, a 2" wide strip, position the 2" mark of the ruler even with the edge just cut, so 2" of plexiglass is covering the cloth. Run the cutter along the edge of the ruler, resulting in a cut strip 2" wide.

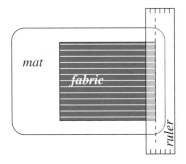

HINT: If you can cut using either hand, this method works well. Simply reverse the ruler-holding hand and the cutter-holding hand for the last step.

If you cannot cut using either hand, however, DO NOT cross your 'cutting hand' over your 'ruler-holding hand'. That is when injuries occur. Either walk around to the other side of the table, placing you in the proper cutting position, or carefully reverse your fabric into the proper cutting position.

General Construction Techniques

Refer to the Table of Contents for specific directions for each pattern in *Scrap Bonanza*. Once the quilt blocks are made, arrange them on the flannel board to determine their final position in the quilt top. Blocks may then be joined to form rows, with rows then being joined to form the quilt top.

Setting Quilt Blocks Together

Before assembling any blocks into a quilt top, double check each one to be sure it is the proper size. If it needs to be trimmed or corrected, it is much easier to do so now rather than rip and repair later.

Even if you only need to trim off a tiny sliver to make the block the proper size, do so. This is what makes the difference between a quilt top that lays flat and one that ripples.

Arrange the blocks on a flannel board. The vertical (up and down) rows will be referred to as row A, B, C, etc. The horizontal rows will be blocks labeled 1, 2, 3, etc.

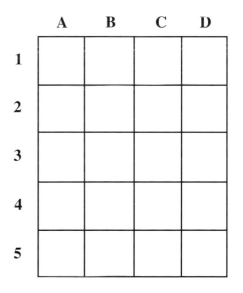

Pinning:

1. In row A, place blocks 1 and 2 right sides together, matching any block seams where necessary, and pin.

2. Add block 3, pinning into position.

3. Continue until the entire A row has been pinned together. Place back on the flannel board, being sure that A1 is at the top.

4. Repeat the pinning process with Row B, placing it in position on the flannel board when pinning is complete, being sure B1 is at the top.

5. Repeat with the remaining vertical rows (C, D, etc.) until all are back up on the flannel board.

Now... do this carefully so you don't confuse the order... remove the rows from the flannel board, beginning with the last row, in order, to the first row (A), stacking the rows so A is on top of your stack. You are now ready to sew.

Sewing:

1. Beginning with row A, stitch blocks 1 and 2 together, placing under the presser foot of the machine so block 1 is on top. DO NOT REMOVE FROM THE MACHINE.

2. In assembly line fashion, insert row B, stitching blocks 1 and 2 together, again positioning so block 1 is on top. Add row C, stitching blocks 1 and 2 together, again with block 1 on top. Repeat until you have added all of your rows. Remove from the machine.

Blocks 1-2 in each vertical row are now stitched together, with a trail of thread temporarily joining the vertical rows together.

3. Go back to row A and begin a new line of stitching. Now stitch blocks 2 and 3 together, with block 2 on top. Insert row B, stitching blocks 2 and 3 together with block 2 on top, and so on, to the end of the stack. Remove from the machine.

4. Go back to row A. Stitch blocks 3 and 4 together, with block 3 on top. Insert row B, stitching blocks 3 and 4 together, and so on.

Joining blocks in this manner links rows A, B, C, etc. with chains of stitching at what will be the points where seamlines will be matched when joining the rows together. It speeds up the assembly process considerably.

5.	When all of the blocks have been stitched into rows, press the rows. This may seem a bit cumbersome, as the quilt top is very 'holey' at this point, but it makes the next step turn out so much better!

6.	Pin Row A to Row B, matching seamlines at the chains of stitching. Stitch.

7.	Pin Row B to Row C, matching as above, and stitch.

8.	Repeat until all of the rows have been joined to form a quilt top. Press.

Borders:

Each quilt shown in *Scrap Bonanza* discusses a different border treatment. Once the quilt blocks have been joined, add the border of your choice. Press.

STORAGE HINT:
If it will be a while before you are ready to sandwich your quilt top, you may want to fold it as few times as possible to hang it on a coat hanger. This will help prevent wrinkles while the quilt top is being stored.

Sandwiching:

1.	Piece fabric as necessary to construct the quilt backing. Backing should be 2" - 3" larger than the quilt top on all sides.

2.	To prepare batting for sandwiching, remove from packaging several hours prior to use so batting may absorb the air that was squeezed out of it in packaging and the fibers may relax. The batting will be much easier to work with. Batting should be 2" - 3" larger than the quilt top on all sides.

3.	Layer backing (wrong side up), batting, and quilt top (right side up), keeping layers taut and smooth as you go, and centering the quilt top so there is an equal amount of excess backing/batting on all sides.

4.	Baste the three layers together to prevent shifting and misalignment as you quilt.

5.	Quilt the three layers of the quilt together.

6.	Trim off excess batting and backing even with the quilt top.

7.	Bind the edges of the quilt.

8.	Attach casings to the back of the quilt if you wish to hang the quilt for display.

9.	Sign and date your quilt.

Sweet dreams!

---

*HINT:	For more detailed information on binding and edge finishing, refer to the Finishing Finesse chapter of "Patches of Time" (see Bibliography).*

Part One:
Stacked Bricks   (cover quilt)

The use of strip piecing and the rotary cutter make this a wonderfully quick scrap quilt. I made my full bed size in three half day work sessions. These instructions give requirements for crib size up through queen size, so you may adjust it according to the size you choose to make, and as all sizes require the same size bricks, you can change your mind halfway through if you like, and make another size.

There are four positions we will talk about in the quilt top:

* bricks (tilted rectangles)
* background (triangles touching bricks)
* lattices (strips between rows of bricks)
* border (consisting of an inner and outer border that frames the entire quilt)

100% cotton prewashed fabrics are recommended for this quilt. You may use scraps in all four positions, or you may take any one of the positions (ex: the background), and use one fabric in that position.

What determines the overall color scheme of this quilt is the color of the lattices.

Yardages are given on page 14. If you choose to use a variety of fabrics for one of these positions, the total yardages should equal the amount shown on the chart. The cover quilt used a golden tan fabric in the background position, and a variety of medium and dark fabrics for the bricks. Be sure to choose brick fabrics that contrast well with the chosen background fabric(s).

The construction technique used here is much like that used in Seminole Patchwork. While the width of the pieces required is listed below, there is no quantity on the number of strips to cut. Because this is a scrap quilt, the number of strips required will vary according to the size of the scraps you are working with.

As with the other quilts in *Scrap Bonanza*, begin by cutting a stack of strips the required size, then begin sewing. After you have some 'bricks' to work with, you will begin to see how well your fabrics are working in combination with each other, giving you a clearer idea of what additional fabrics you will want to cut for the remainder of your quilt.

Cutting: *(1/4" seams included)*

Bricks:
Cut into strips 3 1/2" wide.

*   Use a variety of medium and dark fabrics.   Do not worry about lengths of your strips.   This method utilizes any length.*
*   To achieve a greater variety of bricks, you may want to cut any long lengths of stripping to lengths of about 22". This will allow you to create more fabric combinations with your background fabrics for greater overall variety in your quilt.*

Background:
Cut fabric into strips 2" wide.

*   Do not worry about lengths. Again, this method allows you to use any length.*

Construction of Bricks:

Background and Brick strips are joined to make bands like so:

1.   Place a strip of background fabric right sides together, raw edges even, with a strip of brick fabric. Stitch the matched edge with a 1/4" seam.

When you run out of a strip, just add another and continue piecing, to form one very long band.

2.   Add a strip of background fabric to the remaining long edge of brick fabric in the same manner as above, continuing to add strips when needed to make one very long band.

background

bricks

background

Cutting/Yardage Chart for Stacked Bricks

bed	wall/crib	twin/single	full/double	queen
quilt size	37" x 42"	73.5" x 98"	87" x 98"	96" x 107"
side / foot drop	none	17"	16"	18"
pillow tuck-in	none	6"	7"	9"
total # of bricks	96	456	504	640
# of rows of bricks	6	12	14	16

Cutting lattices and borders: *(1/4" seams included)*

	wall/crib	twin/single	full/double	queen
lattice between rows*	cut 5	cut 11	cut 13	cut 15
	2" x 32.5"	2" x 80.5"	2" x 76.5"	2" x 85.5"
inner border**				
top / bottom	cut 2	cut 2	cut 2	cut 2
	2" x 30.5"	3" x 61.5"	4" x 72.5"	4" x 82.5"
sides	cut 2	cut 2	cut 2	cut 2
	2" x 35.5"	3" x 85.5"	4" x 83.5"	4" x 92.5"
outer border**				
top / bottom	cut 2	cut 2	cut 2	cut 2
	4" x 37.5"	7" x 74"	8" x 87.5"	8" x 97.5"
sides	cut 2	cut 2	cut 2	cut 2
	4" x 42.5"	7" x 98.5"	8" x 98.5"	8" x 107.5"
binding	20" square	28" square	30" square	32" square

> **If purchasing yardage for any of the positions in this quilt, you will need a variety of fabrics that add up to the amounts listed below.**

bed	wall/crib	twin/single	full/double	queen
quilt size (approx.)	37" x 42"	73.5" x 98"	87" x 98"	96" x 107"
bricks	3/4 yd.	2 3/4 yds.	3 yds.	3 3/4 yds.
background	3/4 yd.	2 3/4 yds.	3 1/4 yds.	4 yds.
lattices / inner border	1 yd.	2 1/2 yds.	2 1/2 yds.	5 yds.
outer border	1 1/4 yds.	3 yds.	3 yds.	3 1/4 yds.
binding	5/8 yd.	7/8 yd.	1 yd.	1 yd.

*Before cutting lattices, complete the rows of bricks. Press, taking care not to stretch the rows as you press. Rows may vary slightly in length due to the stretch along the edges of the rows. Find the average length. Cut the lattices between rows this length. See *Join Rows to Lattices* steps 1 - 2 on page 17. Ease rows to fit the lattices, matching midpoints and quarter points as described.

**Before cutting border strips, be aware that these lengths do not allow margins for error or take into account the change in length you may have made on the lattices between the rows due to the stretchiness of the rows. You may want to cut them slightly longer, trimming off any exesss after the pieces are joined.

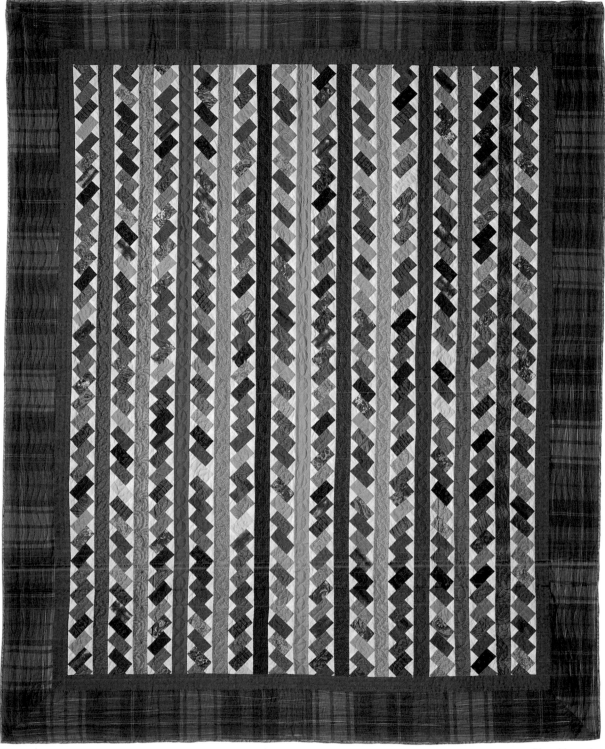

Pieced by author
Quilted by Susan Sterritt

Stacked Bricks

This pattern is ideal for someone new to rotary cutting techniques. The bias edges created along the edges of the vertical rows of bricks ease to fit the straight grain edges of the adjoining lattice strips.

The beauty of this pattern is that even with a wide variety of fabrics used for the bricks, the main color scheme of the quilt is determined not by the fabrics in the bricks, but rather by the fabric in the lattices. It's the perfect pattern for using up lots of odds and ends of scraps.

3. Press the bands, being sure there are no pleats along the seam line. Seams are pressed toward the background fabric. (Traditionally, seam allowances are pressed toward the darker fabric. If you used a dark fabric for the bricks and a light fabric for the background, you will be going against tradition here. Pressing the seams toward the background fabric will give you an important placement guide for joining bricks later on.)

> **HINT:** *Both layers of fabric in a seam allowance are pressed to the same side in quiltmaking so as to seal the seam closed. If the seam was pressed open, the layers of fabric would separate when under stress. This would expose the stitching which would eventually weaken the seam. The open areas along a pressed-open seam are also areas where quilt batting could beard through (migrate up through the opening) and weaken the stitching. For seam strength, press both layers of the seam allowance in the same direction.*

4. Bands are now cut into slices (bricks) 2" wide as shown. Eliminate any slices (bricks) that contain areas where strips abutted together.

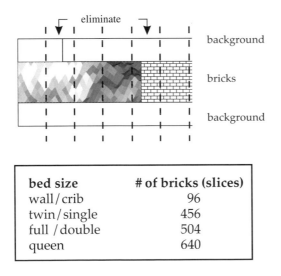

bed size	# of bricks (slices)
wall/crib	96
twin/single	456
full /double	504
queen	640

To Construct Rows of Bricks:

1. To join the slices (bricks), place right sides together, off-setting as shown, so the top of each slice is 1/4" above the seamline of the preceeding slice.

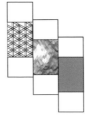

Because of the way you pressed, the top of the slice being positioned will be even with the raw edge of the seam allowance of the slice it is being pinned to.

2. Stitch with a 1/4" seam. Repeat, joining slices into units of two. The units of two may then be joined to create units of four bricks. Fours may be joined to form eights, etc., until you have the required number of bricks in the required number of rows for your quilt.

quilt size	bricks per row	# of rows*
wall/crib	16	6
twin/single	38	12
full/double	36	14
queen	40	16

* NOTE: To add a sense of balance to the quilt, I made half of my rows with bricks slanting in one direction, and half with bricks slanting in the opposite direction.

> **HINT:** *Assembly-line piecing not only saves time, but it also saves thread. After sewing two fabrics together, feed in the next set of two fabrics, without lifting the presser foot. Stitch. Add the next set of two fabrics, etc. Sets will be stitched one after the other forming a long chain of stitched units, each separated by a chain of stitching which later can be clipped.*

3. Press rows using a dry iron. Take care not to stretch the rows as you press.

4. The edges of your rows form a zigzag. Trim off the excess zigzag along the long edges by lining up the 1/4" marking on your ruler with the corners of the bricks. This gives you 1/4" of ruler covering the background fabric beyond the corners of the bricks.

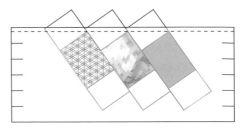

Trim off the fabric that extends beyond the edge of the ruler as shown.

5. The short ends of the trimmed rows are angled. To square off these ends, slice the trimmed row of bricks through the center of one of the bricks, creating a cut that is at right angles to the trimmed edge. (It doesn't matter which brick.)

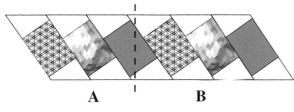

A   B

This splits the row into two pieces. The cut you just made will be the squared-off ends of the row.

6. Reposition the two resulting segments so you may join the angled ends, just as you did when you added bricks to each other.

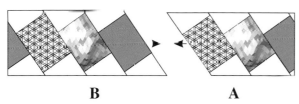

B   A

This will make one long row that is square on the ends.

Joining Rows to Lattices:

* Before cutting lattices, complete the rows of bricks. Press, taking care not to stretch the rows as you press. Rows may vary slightly in length due to the stretch along the edges of the rows. Find the average length. Cut the lattices between rows this length. When performing steps 1-2 below, ease rows to fit the lattices, matching midpoints and quarter points as described.

1. To join the lattices to the rows, fold all strips (bricks and lattices) in half lengthwise to find the midpoint, and again to divide into quarters. Mark the midpoints and quarter points with pins.

2. When joining a lattice to a row, match the midpoints and quarter points. This controls the stretch in the stacked bricks rows. (If you cut lattice strips longer to allow margin for error, take this into account when folding the lattice strip into quarters to mark the midpoints and quarter points.)

3. Join in a row-lattice-row-lattice-row sequence, beginning and ending with a row, until all of the rows have been used. Remember to alternate the direction of the slant of the bricks from row to row.

> **HINT:** *Place pins at a right angle to the cut edge of the cloth. Pin with as small a bite of fabric (amount of fabric 'stitched' onto the pin) as possible. A large bite allows fabric layers to slide up and down the shaft of the pin, losing accuracy.*
>
> *For the best pinning action, use pins no larger around than a size 8 quilting needle. Fatter pins will puncture fabrics.*

4. Press the newly made seams toward the lattices. This reduces bulk and allows the quilt top to lay flat.

Adding Outer Borders :

In order to create the illusion of an outer frame around the whole quilt, each inner border is stitched to its adjoining outer border and added as one unit. Border strips are then mitered in the corners.

1. Join the inner borders for the sides of the quilt to the outer borders for the sides of the quilt, right sides together, raw edges even, midpoints matched, with a 1/4" seam. Press.

2. Repeat with the inner and outer border pieces for the top and bottom of the quilt.

3. Measure the quilt top through the center (A), as shown on page 18, to find the width. Measure the same distance on the top and bottom border bands, spacing evenly around the midpoint.

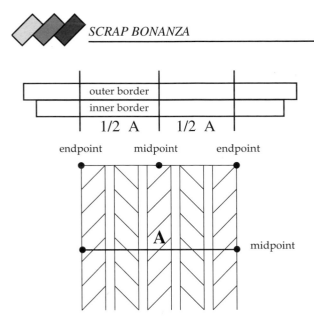

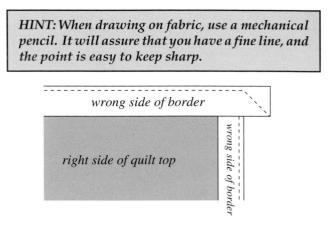

4.   Match the midpoint of the top border band to the top of the quilt midpoint. Match the ends of the quilt top to the pins on the top border band. There will be excess border band at both ends. Stitch with a 1/4" seam, beginning and ending your stitching 1/4" from the raw edge. Repeat with the bottom band.

5.   To attach the side border bands, repeat the procedure, measuring through the center of the quilt lengthwise.

6.   To miter corners, position the quilt top on your work surface so *all borders lay out open flat.* There will be 'tails of border' that overlap in each corner.

7.   Trim off the excess portion of the 'tail' that extends beyond the adjacent border strip.

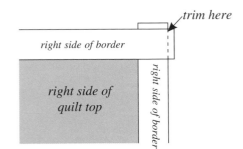

8.   On the wrong side of the border, using a ruler, draw a diagonal line from where your stitching to the quilt top ended to the opposite corner of the overall quilt. Do this on all 8 tails.

9.   Place the tails of the border strips right sides together, raw edges even, and pin, matching the diagonal lines just drawn.

10. Stitch on the diagonal line. Open out the border to make sure the miter is correct and lays flat. Trim off excess seam allowance fabric, leaving a 1/4" seam. Press.

11. Repeat in the remaining corners of the quilt top.

The quilt top is now complete.

Now for the Bonus:

When you are done with **Stacked Bricks**, you will have leftover bricks. Bricks can be combined with additional strips to create a **Glorified Nine Patch**. The number of leftover bricks required for each size quilt is indicated on the **Cutting/Yardage Chart for Glorified Nine Patch.**

Glorified Nine Patch:

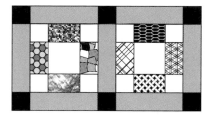

Cutting:

out of medium / dark fabrics:
    cut 2" strips
out of light fabrics (background):
    cut 3 1/2" strips

Each Glorified Nine Patch block requires two leftover brick slices.

Construction:

1. Join the strips as you did for the Stacked Bricks, giving you a striped band:

2. Cut band into 3 1/2" slices.

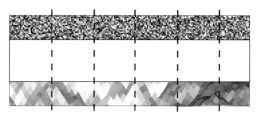

3. Add a brick to both the left and right edges of the 3 1/2" wide slice, resulting in a **Glorified Nine Patch** Block. Press.

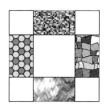

4. The block should now measure 6 1/2" square. It will finish to a 6" square in the quilt. Trim off any excess fabric if necessary to obtain the correct size.

> **HINT:**   *Use the same brand of thread in both the top and bobbin positions. Some brands do not work well with other brands. Different thread brands in these two positions is often the cause of skipped stitches.*

Layout:

Glorified Nine Patch blocks are set together with lattices between each block. A square sits where the lattices intersect. Once the required number of blocks have been made, lay out the blocks on your flannel board, positioning a lattice between each block, with a square where the lattices intersect.

Another use for Stacked Bricks:

Signature Stacked Bricks Quilt:

Many communities are utilizing the 'buy a brick' idea as a way to raise money for a variety of building projects. For a set fee, the sponsor may have their name engraved in a brick that is then used to build the funded project.

Judith Youngman of the Tiadaghton Quilt Guild, Williamsport, PA used this idea with the Stacked Bricks Quilt to raise money for her quilt guild.

Reversing the coloration of the traditional pattern, she used muslin for the bricks and colored fabric for the background. For a set fee, members could sign their name to the muslin for inclusion in the quilt.

Lightly scribing the 3 1/2" wide strip of muslin every 2" (to denote where the cut for the slices would fall, guild members were given boundaries within which to sign their names.

The scribed strip of muslin could then be rolled up and travel from member to member for their signatures, then used as one long segment to construct bricks as previously described.

Cutting/Yardage Chart for Glorified Nine Patch

Finished Block: 6"
Finished Lattice: 1 1/2" wide

bed	wall/crib	lap	twin/single	full/double	queen
quilt size	39" x 46.5"	46.5" x 61.5"	69" x 99"	84" x 99"	91.5" x 106.5"
side/foot drop	none	none	15"	15"	16"
pillow tuck-in	none	none	9"	9"	10"
block layout	5 x 6	6 x 8	9 x 13	11 x 13	12 x 14
total # of blocks	30	48	117	143	168
# of leftover bricks	60	96	234	286	336

Cutting: (1/4" seams included)

	wall/crib	lap	twin/single	full/double	queen
lattices 2" x 6 1/2"	71	110	256	310	362
intersecting squares 2" x 2"	42	63	140	168	195
binding	21" square	24" square	29" square	31" square	33" square

> If purchasing yardage for any of the positions in this quilt,
> you will need a variety of fabrics that add up to the amounts listed below.

bed	wall/crib	lap	twin/single	full/double	queen
quilt size (approx)	39" x 46.5"	46.5" x 61.5"	69" x 99"	84" x 99"	91.5" x 106.5"
light fabrics (background)	1 yd.	1 3/8 yds.	2 3/4 yds.	3 1/4 yds.	3 3/4yds.
medium/dark fabrics (bricks)	1 yd.	1 3/8 yds.	2 3/4 yds.	3 1/4 yds.	3 3/4 yds.
lattices	1 yd.	1 3/8 yd.	2 3/8 yds.	3 yds.	3 3/4 yds.
intersecting sqs.	1/4 yd.	1/4 yd.	1/2 yd.	5/8 yd.	3/4 yd.
binding	5/8 yd.	3/4 yd.	7/8 yd.	1 yd.	1 yd.

Glorified Nine Patch
Leftover brick slices from a **Stacked Bricks** *quilt combine with additional strips of fabric to create this nine-patch variation. Begun as a challenge to make a Stacked Bricks quilt that used only plaids in the brick position, this Bonus Quilt has a totally different flavor from the Stacked Bricks quilt.*

Pieced by author
Quilted by Susan Sterritt

Signature Stacked Bricks
The use of muslin in the brick position provides the perfect spot for signatures for this 'Buy-a-Brick' fund-raiser quilt.

Pieced by Judith Youngman

Flying Geese Variation:

Finished quilt block: 6" square
Unfinished quilt block: 6 1/2" square

The traditional Flying Geese pattern contains 'geese' that are set in vertical rows that run the length of the quilt. A refreshing change of pace from the traditional, this *Flying Geese Variation* is worked in blocks that change position over the surface of the quilt. By joining together a trio of geese, you create a block that is rectangular in shape.

The idea of adding strips to the sides of the block to make it square is something that usually is used as a way to fix a block that wasn't the right size. Done on purpose as a part of the design of the block, it creates a wonderful sense of movement over the quilt's surface.

Flying Geese Variation requires the cutting of two basic shapes: a square and a rectangle. By using a sew-then-cut technique, we will create the units that make up this pattern, as well as units to be used later in the construction of a *Bonus Quilt.*

Begin by dividing your fabrics into 'lights' and 'darks'. 'Mediums' are to be split between the two piles.

While the number of shapes required out of each pile for each size quilt is given on the *Cutting/ Yardage Chart for Flying Geese Variation*, begin by cutting a stack of pieces without counting them.

Construct several blocks as described below, and place them on your flannel board. Observe how the fabrics are working together. Use your observations to determine which fabrics you want to cut into for the remainder of your quilt.

Out of the light pile:
Cut squares: 2 1/2" square

Out of the dark pile:
Cut rectangles: 2 1/2" x 4 1/2"
Cut strips: 1 1/2" x 6 1/2"

Construction:

With ONE dark rectangle and TWO light squares:

1.   Press each small square in half on the diagonal from corner to corner (or draw a diagonal line on each small square, as you choose). It is important that the diagonal marking travel accurately from corner to corner.

HINT: *Placing the square of fabric on a piece of medium-grain sandpaper will keep it from slipping as you draw the diagonal line.*

2.   Position the rectangle horizontally, right side up. Right sides together, raw edges even, place a small square in the upper left corner of the dark rectangle, positioning the marked diagonal as shown.

3.   Stitch through both layers ON THE MARKED DIAGONAL.

4.   In preparation for the *Bonus Quilt*, sew a second line of stitching 1/2" from the first.

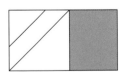

5.   Cut through both layers of fabric midway between the two rows of stitching, resulting in a 1/4" seam allowance for each line of stitching.

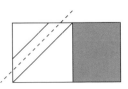

6. Pressing:
    * On the rectangle: press the corner triangle open. This fills in the cutoff corner.
    * On the cutoff unit: press open to create a half-square triangle, pressing the seams toward the darker fabric. Set it aside for use in the *Bonus Quilt*.

7. Repeat steps 2 - 6 in the upper right corner of the rectangle, positioning the square's diagonal from its upper left corner to its lower right corner. Stitch, cut, and press.

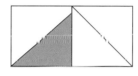

The result:
    ONE Flying Geese Unit
    plus
    TWO half-square triangles

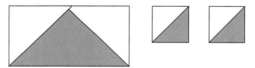

The corner tip of the 'goose' (the beak, if you will) does not hit the outside edge of the unit now. This is correct. Do not think that you have goofed. This is because this block still has its seam allowance on it. When this block is sewn into the quilt top, the tip of the 'beak' will come to the seamline.

Set aside the two half-square triangles for later use in the *Bonus Quilt*.

8. Check the Flying Geese Unit for accuracy. It should measure 2 1/2" x 4 1/2". Trim off any excess fabric if necessary.

Accuracy now will allow you to join the units together later with ease and result in a quilt top that lays flat with no ripples.

9. Repeat the above procedures to create three Flying Geese Units.

10. Join units together to create a trio of geese stacked one above the other, all heading north with 1/4" seams. Press the seams so they too are heading north.

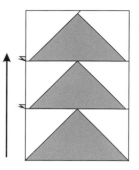

11. Add a dark strip (1 1/2" x 6 1/2") to the left side of the 'trio'. Press the seam toward the added strip.

12. Add a dark strip (1 1/2" x 6 1/2") to the right side of the 'trio'. Press the seam toward the added strip.

PRESSING HINTS:
    * *Work with a dry iron as you press (no steam). Steam can cause the fabric to stretch, distorting the block.*

    * *Press, don't iron. Ironing is when you glide the iron back and forth over the surface. This can stretch the fabric. Pressing is when you hold the iron in position, lift, and reposition the iron in a new spot.*

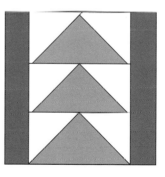

13. You now have a block 6 1/2" square. Check for accuracy. Trim off any excess fabric if necessary.

Cutting/Yardage Chart for Flying Geese Variation Quilt
with 6" borders

Adding borders will provide a deeper drop over the sides of the bed, and a pillow tuck-in. Often times on scrap quilts, the finished border is as wide as one of the blocks, in this case, 6" wide. The chart below includes a 6" border, and lists the amount of quilt that drops over the sides and foot of the bed as well as the amount for the pillow tuck-in.

bed	wall/crib	twin/single	full/double	queen
quilt size	42" x 42"	78" x 102"	90" x 102"	102" x 108"
side/foot drop	none	19"	18"	21"
pillow tuck-in	none	8"	9"	7"
block layout	5 x 5	11 x 15	13 x 15	15 x 16
total # of blocks	25	165	195	240

Cutting: *(1/4" seams included)*

	wall/crib	twin/single	full/double	queen
light fabrics				
2 1/2" squares	150 squares	990 squares	1170 squares	1440 squares
dark fabrics				
2 1/2" x 4 1/2" rectangles	75 rect.	495 rect.	585 rect.	720 rect.
1 1/2" x 6 1/2" strips	50 strips	330 strips	390 strips	480 strips
borders	Cut strips 6 1/2" wide. Join to make the lengths required for chosen size quilt.			
binding	20" square	29" square	30" square	31" square

> **If purchasing yardage for any of the positions in this quilt,**
> **you will need a variety of fabrics that add up to the amounts listed below.**

bed	wall/crib	twin/single	full/double	queen
quilt size	42" x 42"	78" x 102"	90" x 102"	102" x 108"
light fabrics	1 yd.	4 3/4 yds.	5 3/4 yds.	6 3/4 yds.
dark fabrics	1 1/2 yds.	6 3/4 yds.	8 yds.	9 3/4 yds.
border	3/4 yd.	1 3/4 yds.	2 yds.	2 1/2 yds.
binding	5/8 yd.	7/8 yd.	1 yd.	1 yd.

Pieced by author

Flying Geese Variation
*A refreshing change from the traditional Flying Geese,
this variation is set in blocks that change direction
over the surface of the quilt.*

Setting the blocks together:

1. Lay out the blocks in checkerboard fashion, starting with a 'trio heading east' in the upper left corner, alternating the blocks between 'heading north' and 'heading east'. The blocks alternate over the surface of the quilt top.

2. Join blocks to form the quilt top. Press.

Optional Borders:

To add borders:

1. Measure through the center of the quilt lengthwise to see how long the quilt is (including seam allowances.)

2. Cut two border strips this measurement in length.

> **BORDER WIDTH HINT:**
> *Too wide a border can overpower a quilt, while too narrow a border can appear too weak to attractively frame the edges.*
> *Use the finished size of one of the quilt blocks as a guide. The range for the width of your border is anywhere from three quarters to the full width of the block.*
> *Example:*
> *Flying Geese Variation:*
> *6" finished block*
> *Border Width: 4" - 6" wide*

3. Attach these border strips to the left and right edges of the quilt top. Press.

4. To add the top and bottom borders, measure through the center of the quilt widthwise to see how wide the quilt is (including newly added borders).

5. Cut two border strips this measurement in length. Attach these border strips to the top and bottom edges of the quilt top. Press.

Now for your Extra Bonus...

The half-square triangles created in the making of the *Flying Geese Variation Quilt* can now be combined with narrow strips of fabric to create *Split Rail Plus.*

Split Rail Plus:

Ingredients:
* strips of dark fabric: cut 1 1/2" wide

* strips of light fabric: cut 1 1/2" wide

* 3 half-square triangles per block

Units will be joined as shown below:

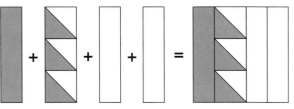

Construction:

1. Join three half-square triangles to form a sawtooth row. Press seams up. This will result in the least amount of bulk at the tips of the triangles.

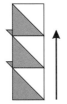

If all of your seams have been an accurate 1/4", the strip will measure 4 3/4" in length.
If your seam allowance was slightly different, you will get a different length.
Record the length you obtain. Work with that length for Steps 2 - 4.

> **HINT:** *For the best accuracy, use the same ruler throughout your entire project. Not all rulers measure the same.*

2. Cut one dark strip the length of your sawtooth row. Join to the left edge of your sawtooth row where shown, with a 1/4" seam. Press the seam toward the added strip.

3. Cut two light strips the length of your pieced strip. Join to the right edge where shown, pressing the seams toward the added strips.

4. Press the block. *The measurement of the resulting square should be the same as the length you recorded in step 1.*

Trim any excess fabric from the strips to make the block square. This adjusts for any variations in your 1/4" seams.

5 Continue making blocks from the leftover half-square triangles from the *Flying Geese Variation Quilt.* Trim all blocks to the same size before joining them together.

Setting the blocks together:

1. Lay out the blocks in checkerboard fashion, starting with a 'horizontal sawtooth' in the upper left corner, alternating the blocks between 'vertical sawtooth' and 'horizontal sawtooth'. The blocks alternate over the surface of the quilt top.

2. Join blocks to form the quilt top.

Optional Borders:

To add borders:

1. Measure through the center of the quilt lengthwise to see how long the quilt is (including seam allowances) .

2. Cut two border strips this measurement in length. *For width of border, see BORDER WIDTH HINT on page 26.*

Example:
   Split Rail Plus:
   4 1/4" finished block
   Border Width: 3 1/4" - 4 1/4" wide

3. Attach these border strips to the left and right edges of the quilt top. Press.

4. To add the top and bottom borders, measure through the center of the quilt widthwise to see how wide the quilt is (including newly added borders).

5. Cut two border strips this measurement. Attach these border strips to the top and bottom edges of the quilt top. Press.

The quilt top is now complete.

> **HINT:** *When choosing thread for your project, a neutral color will eliminate the need to frequently change threads. Thread looks darker on the spool than it does stitched up. A good grouping of thread colors to have on hand for scrap quilts is white, off-white, light gray, medium gray, and dark gray.*

Cutting/Yardage Chart for Split Rail Plus
with 4" border

The block layout and quilt sizes below are the result of the 'leftovers'
from the *Flying Geese Variation Quilt*

bed	wall/crib	twin/single	full/double	queen
quilt size*	38" x 38"	72" x 102"	85" x 97"	93" x 110"
side/foot drop	none	16"	15"	16"
pillow tuck-in	none	11"	7"	14"
block layout	7 x 7	15 x 22	18 x 21	20 x 24
total # of blocks	49 **	330	378***	480

Cutting: *(1/4" seams included)*

light fabrics	Cut in 1 1/2" strips. Refer to directions for length.			
dark fabrics	Cut in 1 1/2" strips. Refer to directions for length.			
borders	Cut strips 4 1/2" wide. Join to make the lengths required for chosen size quilt.			
binding	20" square	29" square	30" square	31" square

If purchasing yardage for any of the positions in this quilt,
you will need a variety of fabrics that add up to the amounts listed below.

bed	wall/crib	twin/single	full/double	queen
quilt size	38" x 38"	72" x 102"	85" x 97"	93" x 110"
light fabrics for block edges	3/4 yd.	4 yds.	4 1/4 yds.	5 1/4 yds.
dark fabrics for block edges	1/2 yds.	2 yds.	2 1/4 yds.	2 5/8 yds.
border	5/8 yd.	1 1/4 yds.	1 1/2 yds.	1 3/4 yds.
binding	5/8 yd.	7/8 yd.	1 yd.	1 yd.

*Fractions have been rounded off to give an approximate quilt size.

** If you use all of the half-square triangles from the *Flying Geese Variation*, there will be one *Split Rail Plus* block left over.

*** If you use all of the half-square triangles from the *Flying Geese Variation*, there will be twelve *Split Rail Plus* blocks left over.

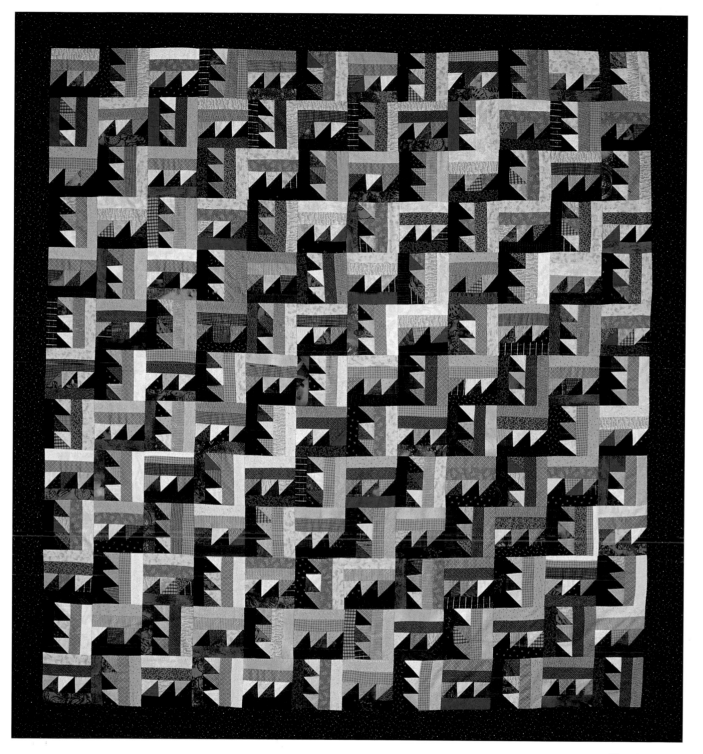

Pieced by author

Split Rail Plus
*Leftover units made in the construction of
the Flying Geese Variation combine with strips of fabric
to make Split Rail Plus.*

Tipped Square, Hidden Star

This pattern is so simple, yet very effective. It uses just squares cut in two sizes. Divide your fabrics into two piles: lights in one pile, and mediums and darks in another pile. For simplicity, the pile of mediums and darks will be referred to as darks. To achieve greater visual interest and richness, remember to vary the scale of design in the fabrics you work with.

While this is a great scrap quilt regardless of the number of fabrics used to make it, the hidden star in this pattern tends to show up best when you choose two colors (such as the tan and blue in the quilt shown on page 32) and work in scraps in that color range. I began with a grocery bag full of tans and another full of blues. Squares were cut as described below to create two basic blocks: a light tipped square with dark corners, and a dark tipped square with light corners. The basic blocks are then alternated over the surface of the quilt top.

Cutting: *(1/4" seams included)*

The total number of pieces required for each size quilt is listed on the chart found on page 32.

Rather than cutting all of the pieces at once, cut a stack of 5" strips (out of both the light and dark piles), then slice those into 5" squares.

Next, cut a stack of 2 3/4" strips (again, out of both the light and dark piles), then slice those into 2 3/4" squares. You are now ready to begin sewing.

As blocks are constructed, position them on your flannel board, alternating the light tipped squares with the dark tipped squares. As you work, see what fabric combinations appeal to you, being sure to maintain a variety of combinations of lights and darks. As you run out of cut squares, cut more to work with until you have the required number of finished blocks.

The leftover cut pieces will be used to create a *Bow Tie Bonus Quilt.*

Construction of Blocks:

1. Press the 2 3/4" squares in half on the diagonal. This crease will serve as a stitching guide.

If desired, rather than pressing the diagonal guide, you may draw in one direction from corner to corner on the wrong side of each square. For ease in drawing, place the square wrong side up on a piece of medium-grain sandpaper.

The sandpaper will grip the fabric as you draw your diagonal line and keep it from stretching or slipping.

Whichever method you choose, be sure your diagonal is accurately placed from corner to corner.

2. Place a small dark square right sides together on top of a large light square, aligned in the upper left corner, with the diagonal guide running from the small square's upper right corner to its lower left corner.

3. Stitch through both layers ON THE DIAGONAL LINE.

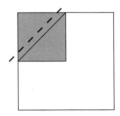

Trim off the excess as shown, resulting in a 1/4" seam.

4. Press open the triangular flap on the light square.

5. Repeat this procedure in each corner of the light square, pressing open each triangular flap as it is added to the large square.

The result is a light tipped square with four dark triangles in the corners.

The tips of the light square will not hit the outside edges of the block. This is correct. This is because the seam allowance is still on the block. When the block is sewn into the quilt, the seam allowance will no longer be visible, and the corners of the tipped square will come to the seamlines.

NOTE: To retain the scrappy nature of this quilt, it is not necessary to use the same dark fabric in all four corners of each large light square.

6. Repeat the above steps to join four light small squares to the corners of each dark large square.

This will result in a large dark tipped square surrounded by four light triangles.

7. Each block should now be 5" square. They will finish to 4 1/2" square in the finished quilt. Check each block for accuracy. Trim off any excess fabric at this point. Accuracy is vital to achieve a quilt top that lays flat with no ripples or puckers.

Setting Blocks Together:

1. To arrange the blocks to form a quilt top, begin with a light tipped square in the upper left corner. Alternate the light and dark tipped squares in checkerboard fashion.

quilt size	# of rows	blocks per row
wall/crib	7	9
twin/single	17	21
full/double	19	21
queen	21	23

2. Step back to get an overall view of the block arrangement. Similar fabrics should be well distributed throughout the surface of the quilt to create the desired effect.

3. Join the blocks to form rows. Press.

4. Join the rows to form the quilt top. Press. Add borders if desired.

Optional Borders:

The width of the borders on the **Tipped Square, Hidden Star Quilt** shown in the photo on page 32 is one half the size of the finished square.

While guidelines for border widths have been given, rules were made to be broken. In this instance, I chose a narrower border so as not to compete with the Hidden Star illusion created by this design.

1. Measure through the center of the quilt lengthwise to see how long the quilt is (including seam allowances).

2. Cut two border strips this measurement in length.

3. Attach these border strips to the left and right edges of the quilt top. Press.

4. To add the top and bottom borders, measure through the center of the quilt widthwise to see how wide the quilt is (including newly added borders).

5. Cut two border strips this measurement. Attach these border strips to the top and bottom edges of the quilt top. Press.

The quilt top is now complete.

Now for the Bonus:

Any leftover squares from the **Tipped Square, Hidden Star Quilt** can be reshaped to use for a charming **Bow Tie Quilt**.

Tipped Square, Hidden Star
To obtain the Hidden Star effect, work in two color groups: one color (a variety of fabrics) for the light position, and a second color (a variety of fabrics) for the dark position.

Pieced by author
Quilted by Susan Sterritt

Cutting/Yardage Chart for Tipped Square, Hidden Star

Finished blocks: 4 1/2"
Border width: 2 1/4"

bed	wall/crib	twin/single	full/double	queen
quilt size	36" x 45"	81" x 99"	90" x 99"	99" x 108"
side/foot drop	none	21"	18"	19"
pillow tuck-in	none	3"	6"	9"
block layout	7 x 9	17 x 21	19 x 21	21 x 23
total # of blocks	63	357	399	483

Cutting: *(1/4" seams included)*

	wall/crib	twin/single	full/double	queen
light fabrics				
5" squares	32	179	200	242
2 3/4" squares	128	716	800	968
dark fabrics				
5" squares	31	178	199	241
2 3/4" squares	124	712	796	964
borders	Cut strips 2 3/4" wide. Join to make the lengths required for chosen size quilt.			
binding	20" square	28" square	30" square	32" square

> **If purchasing yardage for any of the positions in this quilt, you will need a variety of fabrics that add up to the amounts listed below.**

bed	wall/crib	twin/single	full/double	queen
quilt size	36" x 45"	81" x 99"	90" x 99"	99" x 108"
light fabrics	1 1/2 yds.	7 1/4 yds.	8 1/4 yds.	9 3/4 yds.
dark fabrics	1 1/2 yds.	7 1/4 yds.	8 1/4 yds.	9 3/4 yds.
border	1/2 yd.	1 yd.	1 yd.	1 1/8 yds.
binding	5/8 yd.	7/8 yd.	1 yd.	1 yd.

Cutting/Yardage Chart for Bow Tie Quilt

4" finished blocks with 4" border

bed	wall/crib	twin/single	full/double	queen
quilt size	36" x 44"	76" x 100"	84" x 100"	92" x 104"
side/foot drop	none	18"	15"	16"
pillow tuck-in	none	7"	10"	8"
block layout	7x9	17 x 23	19 x 23	21 x 24
total # of blocks	63	391	437	504

Cutting: *(1/4" seams included)*

	wall/crib	twin/single	full/double	queen
light fabrics				
2 1/2" squares	126	782	874	1008
dark fabrics				
2 1/2" squares	126	782	874	1008
1 1/2" squares	126	782	874	1008
borders	Cut strips 4 1/2" wide. Join to make the lengths required for chosen size quilt.			
binding	20" square	29" square	30" square	31" square

> **If purchasing yardage for any of the positions in this quilt, you will need a variety of fabrics that add up to the amounts listed below.**

bed	wall/crib	twin/single	full/double	queen
quilt size	36" x 44"	76" x 100"	84" x 100"	92" x 104"
light fabrics	3/4 yd.	3 3/4 yds.	4 1/4 yds.	4 3/4 yds.
dark fabrics	1 yd.	5 yds.	5 1/2 yds.	6 1/2 yds.
border	3/4 yd.	1 3/8 yds.	1 1/2 yds.	1 3/4 yds.
binding	5/8 yd.	7/8 yd.	1 yd.	1 yd.

Bow Tie Quilt
Cutting leftovers from the Tipped Square, Hidden Star provides pieces needed to make a traditional Bow Tie Quilt.

Pieced by author
Quilted by Susan Sterritt

Bow Tie Quilt

This Bonus Quilt explores another way to use leftover pieces from your first quilt. Cut all leftover 5" squares in quarters, creating 2 1/2" squares.

Each Bow Tie Block uses two light 2 1/2" squares and two dark 2 1/2" squares.

Cut all leftover 2 3/4" DARK squares to 1 1/2" squares.

Each Bow Tie Block uses two dark 1 1/2" squares.

The same construction technique used to create a triangular patch in the corner of a square is used here.

1. Mark one diagonal from corner to corner on the 1 1/2" squares. You may do this by pressing the diagonal in place, or drawing a line on the wrong side of the fabric from corner to corner.

2. Place one dark 1 1/2" square, right sides together, aligned in one corner of a light 2 1/2" square as shown.

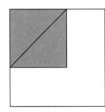

3. Stitch on the diagonal line. Trim away the excess fabric 1/4" beyond the stitching. Press open the triangular patch.

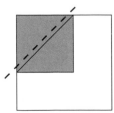

Make two such units for each *Bow Tie* Block.

4. To create a *Bow Tie* Block, join the two light units just made with two dark 2 1/2" squares. The result is a 4 1/2" block.

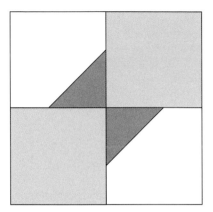

The *Bow Tie* block will finish to a 4" block.

5. Check each block for accuracy. Trim all blocks to 4 1/2" square to correct for any irregularities.

6. Arrange blocks as desired. There are a variety of overall designs that can be created according to how the blocks are positioned. Play with the blocks like a puzzle, and choose your favorite arrangement.

7. Join blocks to form a quilt top. Press.

8. Add borders. Quilt top is now complete.

Weathervane

Strip piecing has never been so effective! The center of each block is made from a 3 1/2" square. All of the remainder of the elements in the block come from strips that have been cut 2" wide.

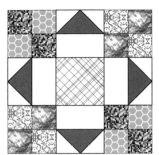

Cutting: *(1/4" seams included)*

As with other quilts in *Scrap Bonanza*, divide your fabrics into two piles, lights and darks. Mediums can go into either pile as described earlier.

Cut a stack of 3 1/2" strips out of dark fabric for the centers of the blocks. Slice strips into 3 1/2" squares.

Next, cut a stack of 2" strips out of both the light and dark piles. You are now ready to begin sewing.

As you construct the units that make up each block, lay them out on the flannel board to judge the overall effect. When you are pleased with the combinations, join the units to form blocks.

Construction of Blocks:

Corner Units: *Each block uses 4 Corner Units.*

1. Place a light strip and a dark strip right sides together, raw edges even. Stitch along one long edge with a 1/4" seam.

When you run out of one strip, simply abut a new strip to it and continue sewing. Make one very long band.

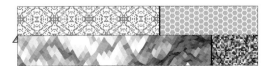

2. Press the seam toward the dark fabric.

3. Slice the band into 2" wide slices.

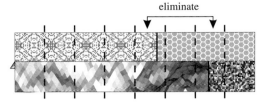

Any slices containing areas where strips were added may be thrown out.

4. Join two slices to make a Four Patch Block. Match seams, and stitch with a 1/4" seam. Press.

5. Unit should measure 3 1/2" square. Check for accuracy. Trim off any excess fabric if necessary.

Triangular Point Units: *Each block uses 4 Triangular Point Units.*

1. Repeat steps 1 and 2 to make a two strip band. Press.

2. Cut the band into 3 1/2" slices. Omit any slices where new strips were added.

3. Out of light fabric, cut 2" squares. Mark one diagonal from corner to corner on the 2" squares. You may do this by pressing the diagonal in place or drawing a line on the wrong side of the fabric from corner to corner.

4. Place one 2" square, right sides together, aligned in one corner on top of the dark strip segment of a 3 1/2" slice.

5. Stitch on the diagonal line. Trim away the excess fabric 1/4" beyond the stitching. Press open the triangular patch.

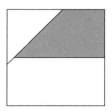

Cutting/Yardage Chart for Weathervane

9" finished blocks
1 1/2" lattices

bed	wall/crib	twin/single	full/double	queen
quilt size	33" x 43.5"	75" x 96"	85.5" x 96"	96" x 106.5"
side/foot drop	none	18"	15"	18"
pillow tuck-in	none	3"	6"	8"
block layout	3 x 4	7 x 9	8 x 9	9 x 10
total # of blocks	12	63	72	90

Cutting: *(1/4" seams included)*

	wall/crib	twin/single	full/double	queen
light fabrics	Cut in 2" strips.			
dark fabrics	Cut 3 1/2" squares for center of blocks (see # below):			
	12	63	72	90
	Cut remainder of dark fabrics in 2" strips.			
lattices	15 @ 2" x 9 1/2"	70 @ 2" x 9 1/2"	80 @ 2" x 9 1/2"	99 @ 2" x 9 1/2"
	4 @ 2" x 44"	8 @ 2" x 96 1/2"	9 @ 2" x 96 1/2"	10 @ 2" x 107"
binding	20" square	28" square	30" square	32" square

> **If purchasing yardage for any of the positions in this quilt, you will need a variety of fabrics that add up to the amounts listed below.**

bed	wall/crib	twin/single	full/double	queen
quilt size	33" x 43.5"	75" x 96"	85.5" x 96"	96" x 106.5"
light fabrics	1 yd.	4 1/4 yds.	5 1/4 yds.	6 1/2 yds.
dark fabrics	1 yd.	3 1/2 yds.	4 yds.	5 yds.
lattice fabrics	3/4 yd.	2 1/2 yds.	2 3/4 yds.	3 yds.
binding	5/8 yd.	7/8 yd.	1 yd.	1 yd.

Weathervane
A combination of speed-piecing techniques creates Weathervane Blocks.
The use of scrap fabrics for the lattices
gives this quilt special flair.

6. Repeat the triangular flap procedure in the other dark corner. Press. This creates a 'Flying Geese' style point.

NOTE: Even though I used several light fabrics for the corner triangular flaps throughout the quilt, I used the same fabric within each Triangular Point Unit. This gave some sense of unity to this design.

7. Each Triangular Point Unit should measure 3 1/2" square. Check for accuracy.

Joining Units:
    Ingredients for each block:
        4 Corner Units
        4 Triangular Point Units
        1 Center Square

1. Lay units on the flannel board to form a block. Play with the units like puzzle pieces, switching around Corner Units, Triangular Point Units, and Center Squares until you are pleased with the result.

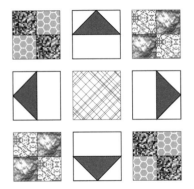

2. Join the units to make a block. Press. Each block should measure 9 1/2" square. Trim off excess fabric if necessary to obtain correct size.

Setting Blocks Together:

1. Arrange the blocks to form a quilt top. Leave room between blocks for the placement of lattice strips.

size	# of rows	blocks per row
wall/crib	4	3
twin/single	9	7
full/double	9	8
queen	10	9

2. Step back to get an overall view of the block arrangement. Similar fabrics should be well distributed throughout the surface of the quilt to create the desired effect.

3. Join the block and lattice units to form the quilt top. Press.

The quilt top is now complete.

Now for the Bonus Quilt:

Leftover Four Patch Corner Units, striped blocks, and plain squares combine for an overall scrap look in *Bits and Pieces*.

Bits and Pieces

The entire quilt is made up of three blocks:

Block A:
a Four Patch

Block B:
a Split Square

Block C:
a full square

Cutting: *(1/4" seams included)*

Divide your fabrics into two piles, lights and darks. Mediums can go into either pile as described earlier.

* Cut a stack of 2" strips out of both the light and dark fabrics for Blocks A and B.

* Cut a stack of 3 1/2" strips out of light and dark fabrics for Block C.

Construction of Blocks:

Block A: working with 2" wide strips:
1. Place a light strip and a dark strip right sides together, raw edges even. Stitch along one long edge with a 1/4" seam.

When you run out of one strip, simply abut a new strip to it and continue sewing.

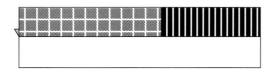

Make one very long band.

2. Press the seam toward the dark fabric.

3. Slice the band into 2" wide slices.

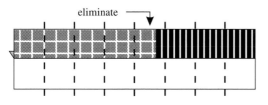

Any slices containing areas where strips were added may be thrown out.

4. Join two slices to make a Four Patch Block. Match seams, and stitch with a 1/4" seam. Press.

5. Unit should measure 3 1/2" square. Check for accuracy. Trim off any excess fabric if necessary.

Block B:
1. Repeat steps 1 and 2 to make a two strip band. Press.

2. Cut the band into 3 1/2" slices. Omit any slices where new strips were added.

Block C:
1. Slice 3 1/2" strips into 3 1/2" squares.

Setting Blocks Together:

Odd rows:

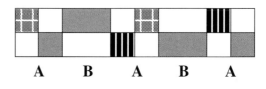

* Alternate blocks A and B, beginning and ending with Block A.

* Place B blocks in a horizontal position.

* Alternate position of light and dark fabrics.

Even rows:

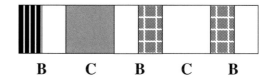

* Alternate blocks B and C, beginning and ending with Block B.

* Place B blocks in a vertical position.

* Alternate light and dark fabrics.

1. Arrange blocks on flannel board as described above until you are pleased with the overall arrangement.

2. Join blocks to form a quilt top. Press.

3. Borders are optional.

The quilt top is now complete.

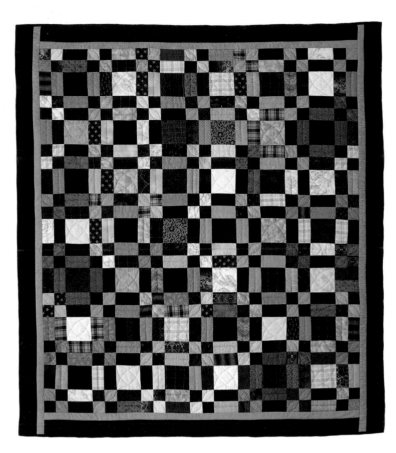

Bits and Pieces
Leftover components from the Weathervane Quilt form an overall scrap quilt very different in flavor from the block and lattice layout of its parent quilt.

Pieced by author
Quilted by Susan Sterritt

Cutting/Yardage Chart for Bits and Pieces
3" finished block with 3" border

bed	wall/crib	twin/single	full/double	queen
quilt size	33" x 45"	75" x 99"	87" x 99"	99" x 105"
side/foot drop	none	18"	16"	19"
pillow tuck-in	none	6"	8"	6"
block layout	9 x 13	23 x 31	27 x 31	31 x 33
total # of blocks	117	713	837	1023
Cutting: *(1/4" seams included)*				
light fabrics	Cut 2" strips.	Cut 3 1/2" strips.		
dark fabrics	Cut 2" strips.	Cut 3 1/2" strips.		
binding	20" square	28" square	30" square	32" square

> **If purchasing yardage for any of the positions in this quilt, you will need a variety of fabrics that add up to the amounts listed below.**

bed	wall/crib	twin/single	full/double	queen
quilt size	33" x 45"	75" x 99"	87" x 99"	99" x 105"
light fabrics	1 yd.	4 yds.	4 1/2 yds.	5 1/2 yds.
dark fabrics	1 yd.	3 1/2 yds.	4 yds.	5 yds.
binding	5/8 yd.	7/8 yd.	1 yd.	1 yd.

The Basic Nine Patch:

1/4" seams used throughout

Tools:
    rotary cutter
    cutting mat
    rotary cutter ruler

Supplies:

thread: Choosing a thread color that blends well with your fabric assortment will prevent the need to change thread colors as you work. Light to medium shades of tan or gray are very versatile and work well for scrap quilts. Use regular dressmaking thread in your sewing machine. Quilting thread is thicker and will throw off the tension in your machine. Save quilting thread for hand quilting.

HINT: Use the same brand of thread for the upper and bobbin threads for best stitch quality. Different brands of thread in these two positions is sometimes the cause of skipped stitches.

---

pins: Slender pins approximately 1" in length work best for matching seams in patchwork. The shafts of longer pins get in the way and reduce your flexibility. Work with pins no larger around than a size 8 quilting needle. Fatter shafts tend to puncture holes in the fabric.

bobbins: Wind two or three bobbins in your choice of thread before you begin. Machine piecing goes through thread quickly. You will be glad for the convenience of pre-wound bobbins.

flannel board: See Part One for a discussion on flannel boards. You will find this an especially helpful tool for working with scrap Nine Patch blocks and the various ways of setting them together.

fabrics: Pull together an assortment of scrap fabrics. Divide fabrics into lights and darks. Medium fabrics can be placed in either pile. If using a medium fabric in a 'light position', place it next to a really dark fabric when stitching. That will make the medium fabric appear lighter. If using a medium fabric in a 'dark position', place it next to a really light fabric when stitching. That will make the medium fabric appear darker.

Scrap Bonanza
Part Two

The Nine Patch

This segment of the book consists of quilts all made with a basic Nine Patch Block. A Nine Patch is a block which is divided into nine equal segments, much like a tic-tac-toe board. It's a great pattern for those new to rotary cutting, as it allows you a chance to create a great quilt while learning new cutting skills.

To test the flexibility of the Nine Patch, I began with a grocery bag full of scraps and constructed Nine Patch blocks until I ran out of fabric. A wide range of speed-piecing techniques provided me with several different 'alternate blocks', each of which changed the overall visual image of the Nine Patch Quilt. The best part of all is that they were all made from scraps on hand.

It's a great way to use up fabric. The freedom of being able to create blocks out of scraps that might not coordinate together in a more rigid format is very rewarding. Several of the 'sets' allowed me to use up larger pieces of fabric on hand and provided the scrap quilt with a 'color scheme' that helped to bind all of the scrap ingredients together into an enjoyable cohesive unit.

In this segment, we begin with Nine Patch Blocks that have a planned color scheme and work our way up to scrap blocks, and even blocks that metamorphosize into new patterns. Working in a series has never been so much fun!

Cutting: *1/4" seams included*

Cut assorted scraps of light, medium, and dark fabrics into strips 2" wide.

To cut fabric into 2" strips:
Begin by straightening one edge of the fabric:

* Fold long pieces of fabric, aligning selvage edges, so the expanse of fabric being cut is in the 12" - 18" range. Place fabric on the cutting mat.

* Position one of the perpendicular lines on the ruler even with the folds, with the edge of the ruler near the raw edge of fabric that needs to be straightened.

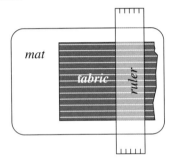

If you are right-handed:
position the edge being straightened to the right (as shown above).
If you are left handed:
position the edge being straightened to the left.

* Hold the ruler firmly in place, keeping finger tips away from the edge of the ruler. To begin your cut, start BELOW the folded edge of the fabric, placing the blade of your cutter along the edge of the ruler, and cut away from you, allowing the blade of the cutter to ride against the edge of the ruler as a cutting guide.

* Now position the 2" mark of the ruler even with the edge just cut, so 2" of plexiglass is covering the cloth. Run the cutter along the edge of the ruler, resulting in a cut strip 2" wide.

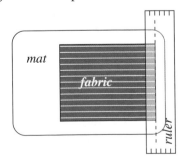

Construction:

1. You now have two piles of strips, lights and darks. Place one strip from each pile right sides together, raw edges even. Stitch along one long edge with a 1/4" seam.

When sewing strips together, as you run out of one strip, abut a new strip to it and continue sewing. Do not piece the scraps together to achieve the needed length, but merely abut them as you sew. These 'joins' will be eliminated in a later construction step.

Sew strips together until you have one very long band.

2. Add strips from the dark pile to the remaining long edge of the light strip with a 1/4" seam, resulting in a three-strip band, as shown below.

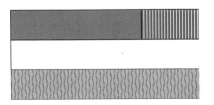

3. Press seams toward dark fabric.

HINT: To press seam allowance toward darker fabric, place unit on ironing board with the dark fabric on top. Peel open the dark fabric, and press along the seamline. This presses the unit from the right side and presses the seam allowance toward the dark fabric all on one step.

4. Construct another series of banding, this time sewing strips together to create a light/dark/light sequence, as shown.

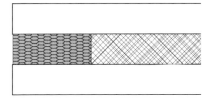

Continue sewing until you have one very long band.

NOTE: *Overall, you will need twice as much footage of dark/light/dark (step 2) as you will of light/dark/light (step 4).*

5. Press seams toward dark fabric.

6. Slice the three-strip bands into slices 2" wide. Eliminate any slices containing abutting edges.

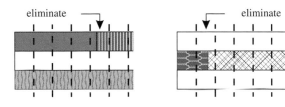

7. Each Nine Patch Block consists of:
   TWO dark/light/dark slices
   ONE light/dark/light slice.

Join slices, matching seams as you sew.

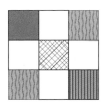

8. Press blocks.

9. Blocks should measure 5" square from raw edge to raw edge. Trim if necessary to obtain the correct size. Accuracy is important if you wish to obtain a quilt that lays flat when the blocks are joined together.

The number of Nine Patch Blocks needed will vary according to the size quilt you are making and the manner in which you choose to join (or set) the blocks together.

Each method of joining is accompanied by a chart listing the number of blocks needed as well as the total yardage for each position in the quilt in case you need to purchase fabric to round out your collection for the construction of the quilt.

Option One:

Block Description:
Two-Color Nine Patch Quilt

Manner of Setting Blocks Together:
Flagstone Alternate Blocks

...Great choice for someone not quite ready to jump into a random scrap project, but prefers quilts with a planned color scheme...

This quilt is not a Scrap Quilt, but rather uses two fabrics throughout the entire quilt: a light fabric in the background position and a medium-to-dark fabric in the other position. Choose fabrics that contrast well with each other.

HINT: Many antique quilts were heavily quilted, not because quilters necessarily enjoyed quilting, but because it was required to hold the batting in place. Without extensive quilting, the batting would fall apart within the quilt when it was washed. To achieve the visual texture of antique quilts without the heavy degree of quilting, choose a light fabric that is a monochromatic print (example: printed muslins, white-on-white prints, ivory-on-ivory prints) for the background position. The quilt shown on page 44 uses a tan-on-tan print in the light position.

Cutting/Yardage Chart for Option One:

Block Description: The Two-Color Nine Patch Quilt   Manner of Setting Blocks Together: Flagstone
Finished Block Size: 4 1/2" square   Border Width: 4 1/2"

bed	wall/crib	twin/single	full/double	queen
quilt size	40.5" x 45"	76.5" x 103.5"	85.5" x 103.5"	94.5" x 103.5"
amount of drop on sides of bed	none	18"	15"	17"
pillow tuck-in:	none	10"	13"	6"
layout of blocks	7 x 8	15 x 21	17 x 21	19 x 21
# of Nine Patch Blocks	28	158	179	200
# of Flagstone Blocks*	32	161	182	203

*four Flagstone Blocks are used in the corners of the border surrounding the quilt

Cutting: *(1/4" seams included)*
Out of light fabric: Cut 5" square for Flagstone Blocks

		32	161	182	203

Remaining light and dark fabrics: cut into 2" wide strips the width of the fabric

Binding:		21" square	28" square	29" square	30" square

> **If purchasing yardage for any of the positions in this quilt,
> you will need fabrics in the amounts listed below.**

bed	wall/crib	twin/single	full/double	queen
quilt size	40.5" x 45"	76.5" x 103.5"	85.5" x 103.5"	94.5" x 103.5"
light fabric (background)	1 3/8 yds.	6 yds.	6 3/4 yds.	7 1/2 yds.
dark fabric	1 3/8 yds.	5 yds.	5 3/4 yds.	6 yds.
binding	5/8 yd.	7/8 yd.	1 yd.	1 yd.

Option One
*Two-Color Nine Patch with
Flagstone Setting*

*The planned nature of this quilt
makes it the perfect choice for
those who are not sure they are
ready to make a scrap quilt
quite yet.*

Pieced by author

Pieced by author   **A**   **B**   Pieced by author

Both quilts are made in Option Two.
One uses a light fabric in the Flagstone position.   *One uses a dark fabric in the Flagstone position.*

Cutting/Yardage Chart for Option Two:

Block Description: All-over Scrap Nine Patch Blocks.
Manner of Setting Blocks Together: Flagstone Blocks with scrap corners
Finished Block Size: 4 1/2" square with Border Width: 1 1/2"

bed	wall/crib	twin/single	full/double	queen
quilt size	34.5" x 43.5"	70.5" x 97.5"	88.5" x 97.5"	97.5" x 106.5"
side/foot drop	none	15"	17"	18"
pillow tuck-in	none	7"	5"	8"
layout of blocks	7 x 9	15 x 21	19 x 21	21 x 23
# of Nine Patch Blocks	32	158	200	242
# of Flagstone Blocks	31	157	199	241

Cutting: *(1/4" seams included)*

For Nine Patch Blocks	light fabrics	Cut into 2" wide strips.		
	dark fabrics	Cut into 2" wide strips.		
For Flagstone Blocks	Cut Flagstone fabric into 5" squares:			
	31	157	199	241
For Border:	Cut Flagstone fabric into 2" wide strips. Piecc to achieve required length.			
For Binding:	21" square	28" square	29" square	30" square

> **If purchasing yardage for any of the positions in this quilt,**
> **you will need a variety of fabrics that add up to the amounts listed below.**

bed	wall/crib	twin/single	full/double	queen
quilt size	34.5" x 43.5"	70.5" x 97.5"	88.5" x 97.5"	97.5" x 106.5"
light fabrics (scraps)	1 yd.	4 yds.	5 yds.	6 yds.
dark fabrics (scraps)	1 yd.	4 yds.	5 yds.	6 yds.
Flagstone fabric (inc. border)	1 1/4 yds.	3 1/2 yds.	4 1/4 yds.	5 1/4 yds.
binding	5/8 yd.	7/8 yd.	1 yd.	1 yd.

Construction:
Option One Nine Patch Blocks:

1. Cut light and dark fabric into 2" wide strips.

2. Place one strip from each pile right sides together, raw edges even. Stitch along one long edge with a 1/4" seam.

When sewing strips together, as you run out of one strip, abut a new strip to it and continue sewing. Do not piece the fabrics together to achieve the needed length, but merely abut them as you sew. These 'joins' will be eliminated in a later construction step.

3. Add strips from the light pile to the remaining long edge of the dark strip with a 1/4" seam, resulting in a three-strip band.

4. Press seams toward dark fabric.

5. Construct another series of banding, this time sewing strips together to create a dark/light/dark sequence.

6. Press seams toward dark fabric.

7. Slice the three-strip bands into slices 2" wide:

Number of slices:		
	light/dark/light	dark/light/dark
wall/crib	56	28
twin/single	316	158
full/double	358	179
queen	400	200

8. Construct Nine Patch Blocks by joining slices like so, matching seams as you join slices:

9. Press blocks. Blocks should measure 5" square from raw edge to raw edge. Trim if necessary to obtain the correct size. Accuracy is important if you wish to obtain a quilt that lays flat when the blocks are joined together.

Number of Nine Patch Blocks:	
wall/crib	28
twin/single	158
full/double	179
queen	200

Flagstone Alternate Blocks:

These blocks are easily made using construction techniques similar to those used in the *Flying Geese Variation Quilt.*

Rather than working with octagons and triangles, the same result can be achieved by using two different size squares:

1. Using light fabric for Flagstone blocks, cut into 5" wide strips.

2. Slice the 5" wide strips into 5" squares.

Number of 5" squares:	
wall/crib	32
twin/single	161
full/double	182
queen	203

3. Out of dark fabric, cut 2" wide strips.

4. Slice the 2" wide strips into 2" squares.

Number of 2" squares:	
wall/crib	128
twin/single	644
full/double	728
queen	812

5. Mark a diagonal from corner to corner of each dark square.

This can be done either by folding the square on the diagonal and pressing or scribing a line on the wrong side of the square. In either case, be sure your marking is accurate and goes from corner to corner.

6. Working with one light (5") square and four dark (2") squares:

Place a dark square right sides together on top of the light square, placing one square in each corner, positioning the diagonals as shown:

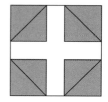

7. Stitch on the marked diagonals.

8. Trim off excess fabric beyond the stitching to achieve a 1/4" seam.

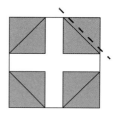

9. Press open the triangular flap in each corner. This turns the trimmed unit back into a square. Each Flagstone block should measure 5" square. Check for accuracy. Trim off any excess fabric if necessary.

Total number of Flagstone Blocks*:	
wall/crib	32
twin/single	161
full/double	182
queen	203

  * four of the Flagstone Blocks are used in the corners of the border surrounding the quilt.

Setting Blocks Together:

1. To arrange the blocks to form a quilt top, begin with a Nine Patch Block in the upper left corner.

Alternate Nine Patch Blocks and Flagstone Blocks in checkerboard fashion.

	quilt blocks per row	# of rows
wall/crib	7	8
twin/single	15	21
full/double	17	21
queen	19	21

2. Join blocks to form the quilt top. Press.

Borders:

The borders on this quilt are made up of bands of dark/light/dark strips joined together in the same manner as for the construction of the Nine Patch Blocks.

1. Measure through the center of the quilt lengthwise to see how long the quilt is (including seam allowances.)

2. Construct two dark/light/dark border bands this measurement in length.

3. Attach these border strips to the left and right edges of the quilt top. Press.

4. To add the top and bottom borders, measure through the center of the quilt widthwise to see how wide the quilt is EXCLUSIVE of the newly added borders. Add 1/2" to this measurement (for seam allowances).

5. Construct two dark/light/dark border bands this measurement.

6. Add a Flagstone Block to both ends of these two border bands. Press.

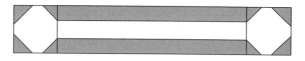

7. Attach these border bands to the top and bottom edges of the quilt top, matching the seams of the border bands to the seams of the borders already attached to the quilt top. Press. The quilt top is now complete.

Option Two:

Block Description:
Scrap Nine Patch

Manner of Setting Blocks Together:
Flagstone: Flagstones are all the same fabric;
   the corner triangles are scrap fabrics

The entire character of quilts made in this option changes according to the color chosen for the Flagstone position. The photos on page 45 show two quilts in Option Two: one with a printed ivory fabric in the flagstone position, for a very traditional look, and one with a dark red print in the flagstone position, creating a strong dramatic look.

Regardless of the fabric choice used, the very nature of this quilt is the combination of fabrics on hand. In order to keep with the scrap bag feel of this quilt, a narrow border was used. This is reflected in the dimensions on the *Cutting/Yardage Chart for Option Two.* If you prefer a wider border for a more generous drop or pillow tuck-in, increase the yardage listed for the Flagstone Fabric as needed.

Construction:

The construction method for this option uses the basic method of Nine Patch construction. All of the Nine Patch blocks are scrap in nature, with no planning as to which color is placed where. Remember that while fabric is referred to as light and dark, you will want to include medium fabrics as well to achieve a quilt that is well-rounded colorwise.

Once the required number of Nine Patch Blocks are constructed, pressed, and trimmed to size, they are laid out on the flannel board in checkerboard fashion, leaving a block's width space in between each block.

The alternate blocks in this option are Flagstone Blocks, constructed as described previously. All of the 5" squares in the Flagstone Blocks are made of the same fabrics (a printed ivory fabric for Quilt A shown on page 45, and a dark red print for Quilt B shown on page 45).

To begin construction of Flagstone Blocks, prepare the Flagstone fabric for rotary cutting, cutting across the width of the fabric. Cut into 5" wide strips. Slice the strips into 5" squares.

The four 2" squares used to form the corner triangles in each Flagstone Block (in both Quilt A and B) are scraps, with a different fabric in each corner position to maintain the scrappy nature of this option.

Once the required number of Flagstone Blocks have been made, they may be added to the arrangement on the flannel board. Stand back to get an overall view of your arrangement. Join blocks to form your quilt top.

The borders shown on Quilt B in this option are 2" strips of the dark red fabric used in the Flagstones. Border strips are cut the length of the quilt top for the sides of the quilt, and the width of the quilt top for the top and bottom of the quilt.

A triangular flap is added to the ends of the border strips in the same method used to create triangular flaps on the Flagstone Blocks. This visually carries the design out into the border and creates a Bow Tie effect as seen below.

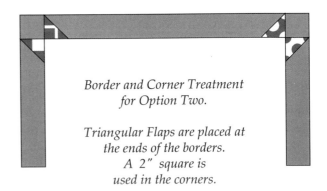

Border and Corner Treatment
for Option Two.

Triangular Flaps are placed at
the ends of the borders.
A 2" square is
used in the corners.

Option Three:

Block Description:
Two-Color Nine Patch
The entire quilt uses the same fabric in the light position. Each Nine Patch Block uses the same fabric in its dark position.

Manner of Setting Blocks Together:
Plain Square
This option is ideal for those who like a little more control over the color placement in their quilt. In effect, it is a 'planned scrap quilt'. The use of plain squares in the alternate block lends to the traditional flavor of the quilt and gives an area ideal for more ornate quilting.

Nine Patch Blocks for this quilt were made in pairs, making two identical blocks at a time. When scattered over the surface of the finished quilt, the like blocks do not jump out.

Construction:

To make two identical blocks:
1. Cutting: light fabric: 1 @ 2" x 14"; 1 @ 2" x 5"
   dark fabric: 1 @ 2" x 14"; 1 @ 2" x 9"

2. Place a 2" x 14" light right sides together with a 2" x 14" dark, raw edges even. Stitch along one long edge with a 1/4" seam.

3. Press seam toward darker fabric. Cut into two segments, one 9" long, one 5" long.

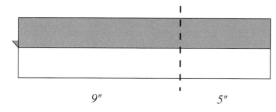

9"   5"

4. Add the remaining 9" dark strip to the 9" long segment to create a dark/light/dark band. Press.

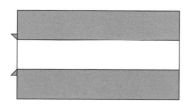

5. Add the remaining 5" light strip to the 5" segment creating a light/dark/light band. Press.

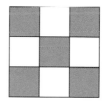

6. Slice both bands into 2" wide slices. There will be some excess band. This is your margin for error.

7. Join slices to make two Nine Patch Blocks. Press. Blocks should measure 5" square. Trim off any excess fabric for accuracy.

8. Construct the following:

Number of Nine Patch Blocks:	
wall/crib:	32
twin/single:	158
full/double:	200
queen:	242
Number of alternate blocks:	**Cut 5" squares.**
wall/crib:	31
twin/single:	157
full/double:	199
queen:	241

9. Arrange blocks in checkerboard fashion, placing Nine Patch blocks in corners. Join blocks to make the quilt top. Press.

10. Borders shown on this option are 4" wide (cut 4 1/2" wide) with a Four Patch in the corners.

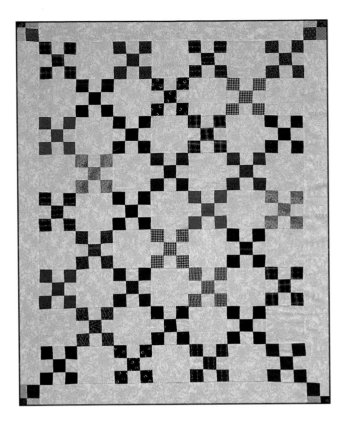

Option Three
Planned coloration gives this a
modified scrap look.

Pieced by author

Cutting/Yardage Chart for Option Three:

Block Description: Nine Patch Blocks: Planned Coloration
Manner of Setting Blocks Together: Plain Alternate Block
Finished Block Size: 4 1/2" square   Border Width: 4"

bed	wall/crib	twin/single	full/double	queen
quilt size	39.5" x 48.5"	75.5" x 102.5"	93.5" x 102.5"	102.5" x 111.5"
side/foot drop	none	18"	19"	21"
pillow tuck-in:	none	9"	8"	10"
layout of blocks	7 x 9	15 x 21	19 x 21	21 x 23
# of Nine Patch Blocks	32	158	200	242
# of Alternate Blocks	31	157	199	241

Cutting: *(1/4" seams included)*
For Nine Patch Blocks   light fabric   Cut into 2" wide strips.
                                        dark fabrics   See directions on page 49.
For Alternate Blocks   Cut light fabric into 5" squares:

31	157	199	241

For Borders: cut 4 1/2" strips. Join to make the lengths required for chosen size quilt.
For Binding: 21" square   29" square   30" square   32" square

If purchasing yardage for any of the positions in this quilt, you will need a variety of fabrics that add up to the amounts listed below.

bed	wall/crib	twin/single	full/double	queen
quilt size	39.5" x 48.5"	75.5" x 102.5"	93.5" x 102.5"	102.5" x 111.5"
light fabric (inc. border)	2 1/4 yd.	6 1/4 yds.	7 1/2 yds.	9 yds.
dark fabric	5/8 yd.	2 3/8 yds.	3 yds.	3 3/4 yds.
binding	5/8 yd.	7/8 yd.	1 yd.	1 yd.

Option Four:

Block Description:
Scrap Nine Patch

Manner of Setting Blocks Together:
Quarter Square Triangles as Alternate Blocks:

Finished Block Size: 4 1/2" square

Quarter-Square Triangles:

The Quarter-Square Triangle blocks used as alternate blocks in this option are constructed in a sew-then-cut method. For this method, there is a 'secret number' used in determining the size of your template. The 'secret number' that will build in the proper seam allowances is **1 1/4"**. Regardless of what size block you are making, add **1 1/4"** **to the finished size** to get the template size for this technique. In this quilt, we are making 4 1/2" blocks, therefore, our template size is 5 3/4" square.

1. Choose two fabrics to be used for the Quarter-Square Triangles. *These fabrics will determine the 'color scheme' of your quilt.* Choose fabrics that contrast well with each other. Fabrics that are too similar will blend together, loosing the optical design this pattern creates.

2. On the wrong side of the lighter fabric chosen, mark squares, 5 3/4" each, as shown.

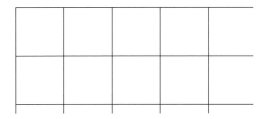

3. Mark diagonal lines from corner to corner of each square. (Each square will now contain an "X")

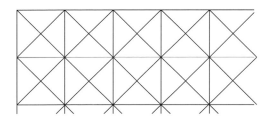

4. Pin fabric RIGHT SIDES TOGETHER with the remaining Quarter-Square Triangle fabric.

5. In EACH square, choose ONE DIAGONAL LINE and stitch through both layers 1/4" on BOTH SIDES of this line.

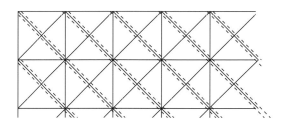

6. Cut through all layers on ALL the pencil lines. Each square will yield the following:

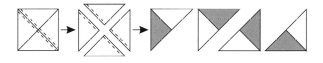

7. Join two of the above units to form a four-triangle-square. Press. Join the remaining two units to form a second four-triangle-square. Press.

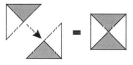

NOTE: Each square drawn on the lighter fabric in step 2 will result in TWO COMPLETED BLOCKS.

8. Each Quarter-Square Triangle block should measure 5" square from raw edge to raw edge. Trim if necessary to obtain the correct size.

9. Nine Patch Blocks are constructed as described previously for scrap Nine Patch Blocks. Divide fabrics into two piles, placing lights in one pile and mediums/darks in the other pile. Cut fabrics into 2" wide strips. Construct Scrap Nine Patch Blocks.

Blocks needed for each quilt size:

	Quarter-Square Triangles:	Nine Patch Blocks:
wall/crib	31	32
twin/single	157	158
full/double	199	200
queen	241	242

Setting Blocks Together:

The intriguing thing about this method of setting blocks together is that a secondary pattern of large stars is formed by the points of the Quarter-Square Triangles.

1. Lay out the blocks in checkerboard fashion, starting with a Nine Patch Block in the corners, alternating the Nine Patch and Quarter-Square Triangle blocks, positioning the Quarter-Square Triangles so large stars are formed. (See photo on page 55)

To obtain the 'star', see the photo on page 55.
    * In one row, the red triangles in the Quarter-Square Triangle blocks are all placed in the north/south positions.

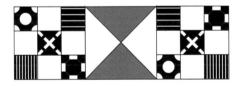

    * In the next row, the red triangles are place in the east/west positions.

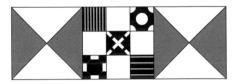

    * The positions of the red triangles alternate from row to row, running north/south all the way across one row, running east/west all the way across the next row, and so on..

2. Join blocks to form the quilt top, matching block seams as you stitch. Press.

Borders:

The borders on the quilt shown consist of two strips that have been sewn together. The inner border is 2 1/2" wide, the outer border is 3" wide. The *Cutting/Yardage Chart for Option Four* will tell you the lengths needed for the various size quilts.

1. To create the borders, join the inner and outer border strips with a 1/4" seam. Press. Repeat with the remaining strips for a total of four border bands.

2. To add borders, measure through the center of the quilt lengthwise to see how long the quilt is (including seam allowances). Cut two border bands this measurement. Attach these border bands to the left and right edges of the quilt top with a 1/4" seam. Press.

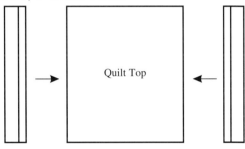

3. To add the top and bottom borders, measure through the center of the quilt widthwise to see how wide the quilt is (including the newly added borders). Cut the two remaining border bands this measurement.

4. To complete the quilt top, attach these border bands to the top and bottom edges of the quilt top with a 1/4" seam. Press.

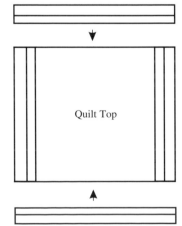

Other Uses For Quarter-Square Triangles:

The technique of setting quilt blocks with an alternate block of 'Quarter-Square Triangles' is a very useful one. In terms of construction, it is a fast way to make half the blocks needed for the quilt top.

Visually, it creates the illusion of framing each quilt block with a tipped square. This is especially appropriate for *sampler quilts* where a unifying factor is needed to link all of the blocks into a cohesive quilt. It also works well when a *limited number of blocks* is not sufficient to make a quilt as large as you would like it to be.

The *Schoolhouse Revisited Quilt* shown on page 58 was set together with Quarter-Square Triangles as the alternate block. Although each house is different, they blend well in this quilt due to the unifying factor of the Quarter-Square Triangles. While the framed blocks appear to be 'set on point', they are actually set together in very simple vertical and horizontal rows.

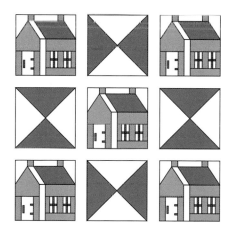

The use of 'Quarter-Square Triangles' as the setting block *defines the color scheme of a quilt.* Even though the Nine Patch blocks used in the quilt on page 55 are made of hundreds of multicolored scraps, the overall quilt appears to be red and blue due to the use of those colors as the Quarter-Square Triangles.

The key points to remember when making Quarter-Square Triangle blocks are:

* Determine the finished block size. To this, add 1 1/4" to obtain the template size needed for this technique.

Examples: 3" finished block
     4 1/4" square template

     6" finished block
     7 1/4" square template

     9" finished block
     10 1/4" square template

* Each template marked on the fabric will result in TWO completed Quarter-Square Triangle blocks.

* After each block is completed and pressed, it will contain the 1/4" seam allowance required on all four edges. The size now will be 1/2" larger than the finished block size.

Examples: 3" finished block
     3 1/2" pressed size

     6" finished block
     6 1/2" pressed size

     9" finished block
     9 1/2" pressed size

Check all blocks for accuracy. Trim off any excess fabric if necessary.

Cutting/Yardage Chart for Option Four

Block Description: Scrap Nine Patch Blocks   Manner of Setting Blocks: Quarter-Square Triangle Blocks
Finish Block Size: 4 1/2 square   Borders: All sizes have a 4 1/2" non-mitered border surrounding the quilt

bed	wall/crib	twin/single	full/double	queen
quilt size	40.5" x 49.5"	76.5" x 103.5"	94.5" x 103.5"	103.5" x 112.5"
side/foot drop	none	18"	20"	21"
pillow tuck-in	none	10"	8"	11"
layout of blocks	7 x 9	15 x 21	19 x 21	21 x 23
# of Nine Patch blocks	32	158	200	242
# Quarter-Sq. Triangle blks.	31	157	199	241

Cutting for Borders: uses Quarter-Square Triangle fabrics: *(1/4" seams included)*

	wall/crib	twin/single	full/double	queen
For outer border	4 @ 3" x 43"	4 @ 3" x 97"	4 @ 3" x 97"	4 @ 3" x 106"
For inner border	4 @ 2.5" x 43"	4 @ 2.5" x 97"	4 @ 2.5" x 97"	4 @ 2.5" x 106"
binding	21" square	28" square	29" square	30" square

> **If purchasing yardage for any of the positions in this quilt, you will need a variety of fabrics that add up to the amounts listed below.**

bed	wall/crib	twin/single	full/double	queen
quilt size	40.5" x 49.5"	76.5" x 103.5"	94.5" x 103.5"	103.5" x 112.5"
yardage for Scrap Nine Patch Blocks				
light fabrics	1/2 yd.	2 yds.	2 1/2 yds.	3 yds.
dark fabrics	5/8 yd.	2 1/2 yds.	3 yds.	4 yds.

yardage for Quarter-Square Triangles: uses TWO fabrics in the following amounts:

	1 1/2 yds. ea.	3 yds. ea.	3 1/2 yds. ea.	4 yds. ea.
binding	5/8 yd.	7/8 yd.	1 yd.	1 yd.

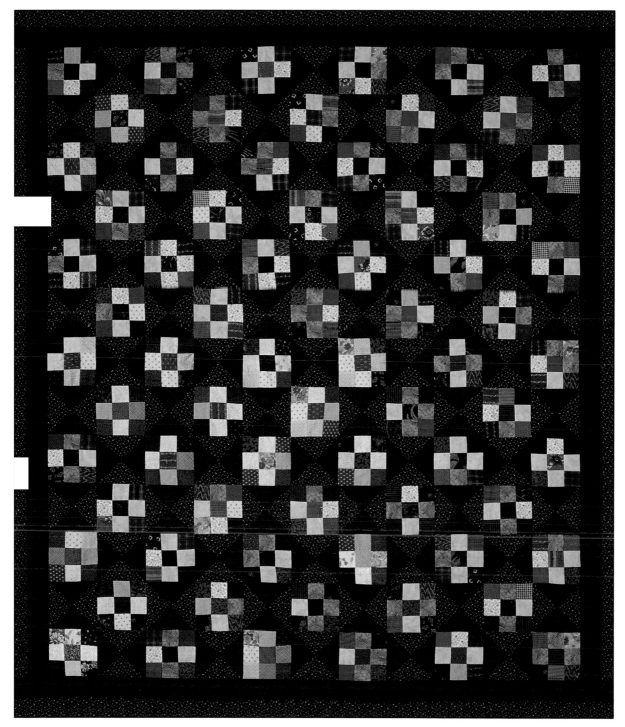

Option Four:
Scrap Nine Patch with Quarter-Square Triangles

The use of Quarter-Square Triangles determines the color scheme
of the overall quilt as well as creates
a secondary pattern.

Option Five:

Block Description:
Scrap Nine Patch Blocks that change into Shoofly Blocks as they travel over the surface of the quilt

Manner of Setting Blocks Together:
Lattices with squares at intersections

This quilt started out as Scrap Nine Patch blocks set together with lattices. As I began laying blocks out on the flannel board, I began to wonder what other speed piecing techniques I could use on the Nine Patch to get a new pattern.

The same technique which began in the *Flying Geese Variation* was used in the corners of these Nine Patch blocks to transform them into a popular pattern called the *Shoofly*.

To make the pattern transition, I began laying out Nine Patch blocks in the lower left corner of the flannel board. As I traveled diagonally up toward the upper right corner, I began adding corner triangles to the Nine Patches. Some blocks have one corner triangle, some have two, some have three, and some have four, so that by the time I arrived in the upper right corner, I was working with Shoofly Blocks.

I call this quilt *Metamorphosis*. I love the way it begins as one traditional pattern and blossoms into another.

The use of plaid fabric in the border of this quilt helps to pick up several of the colors within the Nine Patch blocks and unify them.

Construction:

1.   Divide scrap fabrics into two piles. Place light fabrics in one pile. Place dark fabrics in another pile. Medium fabrics can go into both piles. Remember to vary the scale of design on your printed fabrics when working on a scrap quilt.

2.   Cut fabrics into strips 2" wide.

3.   Construct scrap Nine Patch blocks as described previously.

quilt	# of Scrap Nine Patch Blocks
wall / crib	30
lap	48
twin / single	176
full / double	208
queen	255

4.   To transform blocks: cut a 2" square for each corner being transformed. Mark a diagonal from corner to corner on the 2" square.

5.   Place the marked square right sides together with the Nine Patch Block, aligning corners.

6.   Stitch on the marked diagonal.

7.   Trim away excess fabric beyond the stitching so as to form a 1/4" seam.

8.   Press open the triangular flap in the corner.

9.   Repeat in as many corners as desired to make the transformation into a *Shoofly Block.*

Setting Blocks Together:

Refer to the photo on page 59 to see how blocks transform over the quilt surface from a *Nine Patch* block into a *Shoofly* block. Lattices are positioned between blocks, with a contrasting square placed at each intersection. The contrasting squares in this quilt are a variety of scraps.

Join quilt blocks and lattices to form the quilt top. Press.

Borders:

The borders on this quilt are made up of plaid fabric cut in 3" wide strips, with a 3" contrasting square in each corner.

1.   Measure through the center of the quilt lengthwise to see how long the quilt is (including seam allowances).

2.   Cut two borders this length by 3" wide.

3.   Attach these border strips to the left and right edges of the quilt top. Press.

4.   To add the top and bottom borders, measure through the center of the quilt widthwise to see how wide the quilt is EXCLUSIVE of the newly added borders. Add 1/2" to this measurement (for seam allowances).

5.   Cut four 3" squares to be used in the corners of the quilt.

6. Add a 3" square to both ends of these two strips. Press.

7.   Attach these border bands to the top and bottom edges of the quilt top, matching the seams of the border bands to the seams of the borders already attached to the quilt top. Press.

The quilt top is now complete.

Pieced by Judith Youngman
Quilted by Lola McCarty

Schoolhouse Revisited
*from the cover of **Patches of Time** by the author © 1991*

Quarter-Square Triangles make the perfect alternate block setting
for a variety of quilt blocks, as seen here
in Schoolhouse Revisited.
*Pattern given in **Patches of Time***

Option Five:
Metamorphosis

What starts as a Scrap Nine Patch blossoms into a Shoofly as the blocks travel over the quilts surface. The use of multi-colored scraps for the lattice intersections lends a jeweltone effect to the quilt.

Pieced by author

Cutting/Yardage Chart for Option Five

Finished Block: 4 1/2"   Lattice: 1 1/2" wide   Border: 2 1/2" wide

bed	wall/crib	lap	twin/single	full/double	queen
quilt size	31.5" x 37.5"	37.5" x 49.5"	72.5" x 102.5"	84.5" x 102.5"	96.5" x 108.5"
side / foot drop	none	none	16"	15"	18"
pillow tuck-in	none	none	11"	12"	10"
block layout	5 x 6	6 x 8	11 x 16	13 x 16	15 x 17
total # of blocks	30	48	176	208	255

Cutting: *(1/4" seams included)*

	wall/crib	lap	twin/single	full/double	queen
lattices (2" x 5")	71	110	379	445	542
intersecting squares (2" x 2")	42	63	204	238	288
borders	Cut fabric into 3" wide strips. Piece to achieve required length.				
binding	21" square	24" square	29" square	31" square	33" square

> **If purchasing yardage for any of the positions in this quilt,**
> **you will need a variety of fabrics that add up to the amounts listed below.**

bed	wall/crib	lap	twin/single	full/double	queen
quilt size (approx)	31.5" x 37.5"	37.5" x 49.5"	72.5" x 102.5"	84.5" x 102.5"	96.5" x 108.5"
light fabrics	1 yd.	1 3/8 yds.	2 3/4 yds.	3 1/4 yds.	3 3/4 yds.
medium / dark fabrics	1 yd.	1 3/8 yds.	2 3/4 yds.	3 1/4 yds.	4 yds.
lattices	1 yd.	1 3/8 yd.	3 yds.	3 1/2 yds.	4 yds.
intersecting sqs.	1/4 yd.	1/4 yd.	3/4 yd.	7/8 yd.	1 yd.
border	1/2 yd.	3/4 yd.	1 1/4 yds.	1 1/2 yds.	1 5/8 yds.
binding	5/8 yd.	3/4 yd.	7/8 yd.	1 yd.	1 yd.

Scrap Potpourri:

Speed Piecing Techniques combine with scraps to make up this mini-quilt. The blocks have been scaled down to 3" finished blocks, in part because I still had some scraps left over that I couldn't resist making some good use of.

The techniques used, as well as the dimensions needed to obtain a 3" finished block, are given below. Yardages are not listed for this sampler because it really is a scrap bonanza.

Feel free to play and experiment. The possibilities for mosaic intrigue are endless. It is what keeps us all so fascinated with patchwork.

Scrap Nine Patch Blocks:

Cut strips 1 1/2" wide. Construct Nine Patch Blocks. Press. Trim to 3 1/2" square.

Shoofly Blocks:

Cut strips 1 1/2" wide for construction of a basic Nine Patch Block.

Use 1 1/2" squares in the corners to transform the block into a *Shoofly* as on page 56. Press. Trim to 3 1/2" square.

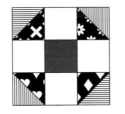

Quarter Square Triangles:

The finished block is 3". Using the 'magic number' for this technique of 1 1/4", the template size required is 4 1/4" square. Construct Quarter-Square Triangle Blocks as described on page 51. Press. Trim to 3 1/2" square.

Remember that for EACH 4 1/4" square you draw on your fabric, you will end up with TWO finished blocks.

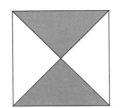

Windmill Blocks:

These are made of four Half-Square Triangles sewn together to make a 3" block. Each Half-Square Triangle unit, then, finishes to 1 1/2".

Half-Square Triangle Unit

Half-Square Triangle blocks are made in a sew-then-cut method similar to Quarter-Square Triangles. In this case, the 'magic number' is 7/8". The template required then is 1 1/2" + 7/8", or 2 3/8".

1. Choose two fabrics to be used for the Half-Square Triangles. Choose fabrics that contrast well with each other. Fabrics that are too similar will blend together, loosing the optical design this pattern creates.

2. On the wrong side of the lighter fabric chosen, mark squares, 2 3/8" each, as shown.

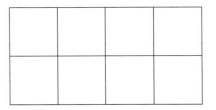

3. Mark diagonal lines from corner to corner of each square IN ONE DIRECTION ONLY.

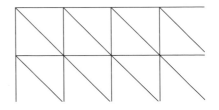

4. Pin fabric RIGHT SIDES TOGETHER with the remaining Half-Square Triangle fabric.

5.   In EACH square, stitch through both layers 1/4" on BOTH SIDES of the diagonal line.

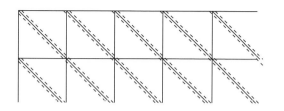

6.   Cut through all layers on ALL the pencil lines. Each square will yield the following:

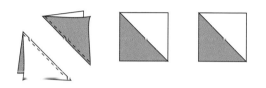

7.   Join four half-square triangle units together to make a *Windmill Block*.

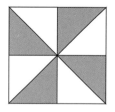

Block Layout:

As this is a *Scrap Potpourri*, feel free to use any combination of blocks. I built my block arrangement similar to the Barn Raising Layout used in Log Cabin Quilts, with a *Shoofly* in the center, surrounded by *Scrap Nine Patch* blocks, surrounded by *Windmills*, with *Scrap Nine Patch* blocks in the corners. The Alternate Block positions were filled in with *Quarter-Square Triangle* blocks.

Place blocks on the flannel board in the arrangement of your choice. Join blocks to make a quilt top. Borders are optional. Press.

The quilt top is now complete.

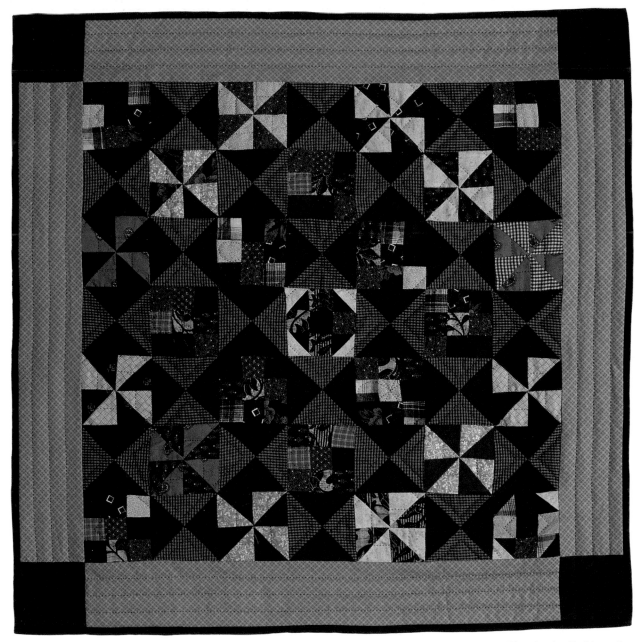

Scrap Potpourri
block size: 3″

A variety of speed piecing techniques are used to create Scrap Potpourri :
Half-Square Triangles
Quarter-Square Triangles
Scrap Nine Patch Blocks
Shoofly

About the Author

Linda Halpin began sewing at the age of 6. By the time she discovered quilting, she had a healthy supply of scraps just waiting to become quilts. Her interest in quilting has led her down many paths, from history and folklore, to dimensional appliqué, to clothing, and, of course, to scrap quilts.

Linda has been actively teaching quiltmaking across the United States and Canada for 19 years. Certified by the Embroiderer's Guild of America (EGA) as an Instructor in Quiltmaking, she has served as past EGA Chairman of the Master Craftsman Program for Quiltmaking and the Teacher Certification Program.

"Quiltmaking never fails to fascinate me. There are always exciting things to learn, new avenues to explore, more fabric waiting to be purchased."

Linda makes her home with her patient husband, two wonderful children, a very friendly beagle, and two parakeets in Reedsburg, Wisconsin.

Other Books by Linda Halpin

Patches of Time   1991

A collection of traditional patterns each ranging from crib to queen size, are accompanied by chapters on the history and folklore behind the design. Included are quilting patterns and a chapter on Finishing Finesse.   112 pages

Appliqué a la Mode   1992

A workbook for Baltimore Album Floral Techniques, *Appliqué a la Mode* includes three dimensional blossoms, woven basket techniques, and sawtooth edgings, as well as the history behind such techniques being used on quilts.   32 pages

Beyond the Bog Coat   1993

Patterned to your measurements, the Bog Coat's ethnic simplicity adapts well to any shape. Clothing design and such quiltmaking embellishments as Seminole Patchwork, Stripping, Curved Strip Piecing, Piping, Appliqué Overlays, and Pleating are explored in this garment design workbook.   32 pages

These books are available from your favorite quilt shop, or may be ordered directly from the publisher.

RCW Publishing

RR #3 Old Post Lane   Columbia Cross Roads, PA   16914-9535
717-549-3331

Bibliography

Scrap Quilts:

Beyer, Jinny
The Scrap Look
EPM Publications, Inc.
McLean, VA 22101
© 1985

Martin, Judy
Scrap Quilts
Moon Over the Mountain Publishing Co.
Wheatbridge, CO 80033
© 1985

Martin, Judy
Scraps, Blocks & Quilts
Crosley - Griffith Publishing Co., Inc.
Denver, CO 80215
© 1990

Quilting:

Hargrave, Harriet
Heirloom Machine Quilting
C & T Publishing
Lafayette, CA 94549
© 1990

Leone, Diana
Fine Hand Quilting
Leone Publications
Los Altos, CA
© 1986

Marston, Gwen & Cunningham, Joe
Quilting With Style
American Quilter's Society
Paducah, KY
© 1993

Simms, Ami
How To Improve Your Quilting Stitch
Mallery Press
Flint, MI
© 1987

Finishing:

Dietrich, Mimi
Happy Endings
That Patchwork Place, Inc.
Bothell, WA
© 1987

Halpin, Linda
Patches of Time
RCW Publishing Company
Columbia Cross Roads, PA
© 1991